WATCH ME DIE

LAST WORDS FROM DEATH ROW

BILL KIMBERLIN, Psy.D

WILDBLUE
PRESS

WildBluePress.com

WATCH ME DIE published by:
WILDBLUE PRESS
P.O. Box 102440
Denver, Colorado 80250

ISBN 978-1-952225-84-0 Trade Paperback
ISBN 978-1-952225-83-3 eBook

Cover design © 2021 WildBlue Press. All rights reserved.

Interior Formatting/Cover Design by Elijah Toten
www.totencreative.com

WATCH ME DIE

Table of Contents

PROLOGUE

May 24, 2007

I woke up at 2:30 a.m. I wouldn't really say I woke up since I haven't really slept the past week anyway, too much going through my mind. What will it be like? Will it hurt? Is there suffering? What happens when it's all over? Will I get sick or cry just before it is done? Less than eight hours from now I will be locked in the death house at Southern Correctional Institute, in Lucasville, Ohio, one of the toughest prisons in the state and the only one to perform executions. What should I do to prepare? Why worry? I just need to do whatever the prison staff and guards tell me to do. I have no choice in this matter. All I really need to do is to prepare myself mentally for this date with death.

I shower and shave. I try to look my best for whomever shows up to the spectacle. I skipped my breakfast because I'm too afraid I will not be able to keep it down. Plus, who could have an appetite when only hours from now, death's doorbell will be ringing? I hate the thought of being paraded around in front of all of these people from the media. Wondering what they are going to write about me when this is all over with. Knowing they never report the actual facts.

The prison staff and guards are much nicer to me than they normally are. It must be because of what's about to happen. I'm not sure if they feel sorry for me or if they just enjoy looking at the blank, uncertain stare in my eyes. The guards walked me through the process. I know they are talking directly to me, but I can't really register what they are saying. Everything seems like a blur. All of the talking going on around me seems to run together. It's hot in here since 80 °F outside of the prison walls makes it feel like 100 °F in here. The rest of the prison is on lockdown, or what the administration calls Restrictive Movement. The inmates are restless; and as I am led to the death chamber, I can hear them yelling and screaming. I don't know what they are saying, but I do know that some of them are yelling at me.

I glance over and I can see the hearse sitting outside of the death house. This can't be real! It looks as though the hearse is from an old western movie set. The driver looks like he is from the movie *Deliverance*! I'm walked right in front of the media, to the death house. I can feel their stares. They glance at me and whisper to each other as they write their notes about me on their cheap office issued notepads.

The time has flown by. I'm sweating now. It seems like it was less than a minute ago that I was getting up at 2:30 a.m. It's now 9:50 a.m. In just ten minutes the first needle will be inserted to start this legal homicide that people have gathered around to see. I know I'm breathing because I can feel my heartbeat. I try to look calm and composed. I don't want these people to think for one minute that I am nervous or afraid of what is about to take place. Why should I care about what the so-called journalists think about me anyways? I'm never going to see them again. They've already asked me if I wanted to give them a statement and I refused. This all seems so surreal. In just a few short minutes, a human life will be taken while people watch like it is some sort of freak show. How can this be in our civilized society today in the most industrialized nation on Earth?

The warden asks for a final statement before the process begins. With a single motion of buttoning his suit jacket, the warden just invited death in. Death is hovering in the death chamber, and so many things are going through my mind.

It is so quiet that I can hear my heart in my throat, and I wonder if anyone else can hear it. There is no turning back now as the first of three drugs travel through tubes and into veins. I wonder what everyone else is thinking right now. Most of all, I wonder what the condemned man strapped to the deathbed by six straps is thinking. You see, I am just a witness to the execution. I am just one of a group sitting a couple of feet away watching this life being taken. He is experiencing it! What does it feel like? Does it hurt? What happens when it's all over?

CHAPTER 1

HOW IT ALL BEGAN

People ask me all the time, "Bill, how on earth did you ever decide to study death row and why?" Well, the simple answer would be that it needed to be done; but of course just like in life, there are no such things as simple answers. With that said, I will try not to bore you with my answer, even though I believe it is extremely important to explain how this journey began.

I had always wanted to become a college professor. While I was an adult probation officer in Ohio, I decided to go for my graduate degree and then on to get my doctorate. It has always been said that you needed those little letters before and after your name to teach college full time. However, based on my years of experience now, I can say with complete certainty that nothing could be farther from the truth. It is really based on who you know, not what you have accomplished.

During graduate and postgraduate courses, the realization came that many of my professors were what is called *book smart* and were really only teaching from those books. They studied books, wrote papers on those subjects, and then considered themselves experts in the field. One professor had written a book, required for class, about drug usage and the ethics of drug legalization. He sounded very knowledgeable in the subject; however, when types of drugs and their effect on society were discussed, the realization came that this professor had never even seen crack cocaine firsthand, or heroin. He had never visited places like Amsterdam where the drug laws are extremely relaxed. Everything he was teaching had been learned from other books. His expectations were for students to write an educated opinion on a subject based on his expertise which had come only from other books with no life experiences. Immediately, the decision was made to never become that type of professor.

Now I know that you can't be an expert on everything, and I also know that you don't have to experience everything in order to teach about it. I've never experimented with drugs, yet I have counseled hundreds of addicts over the years. Still, while my expertise in some areas of the social sciences falls just short of personal experience, I have gone to great lengths to ensure that I have as much knowledge as possible in those areas before teaching them. I've never given birth and have not experienced the pain, yet I was there throughout my wife's pregnancy and the birth of our son, allowing me to explain the process firsthand, which I do every semester in my human growth and development courses.

Good students will often challenge their professors on particular subjects to discover what their stance is. In my fields of study, there are four subjects which consistently cause debate and heated arguments. They are abortion, gun rights, the legalization of drugs, and capital punishment. I have been to abortion clinics and witnessed firsthand what the women go through psychologically before and after they make such a life-altering decision. I also come from a family where before you leave the hospital after you are born, family members are deciding what gun to get you for your first Christmas. I've traveled to other countries, including Holland, to see how those societies deal with relaxed or legalized drug policies. While I do not in any way consider myself an expert in these fields, I do believe that when I teach them, or when asked about these topics, I can offer an educated opinion that goes above and beyond what I have read in a book or what I have been told by someone else.

Whenever the topic of capital punishment or death row came up, I felt frustrated. Speaking for or against the death penalty was difficult because everything I knew about it came from newspapers, books, non-criminal people, or worse yet, television! This was when I decided to go see what an execution was like in person. How difficult could that be to set up, right? I never expected that it would take eight years to be able to tell what I had discovered.

In 2007, with the help of one of my closest friends, Roger Binette, who happened to be an Assistant County Prosecutor at the time and is now a Common Pleas Court judge in Erie County, Ohio, I set out on this escapade to see what I could learn. Roger was able to get me some contact numbers for the Attorney General's office, and so I called them. I spoke with an assistant and asked her if she could put me on a list to witness an execution. She laughed and then somehow our phone call got disconnected. I like to think it was due to a bad phone connection, but realistically, I think she hung up on me. I decided to give it another try, and I called her back. I explained to her who I was and why I needed to witness an execution as part of my research on death row. I think she felt sorry for me because she explained that there are 80 million residents in the state of Ohio and only three people on each side ever get to witness an execution. In fact, she told me the Attorney General herself had never even witnessed an execution before.

The Ohio Revised Code, which contains all of the current statutes of the Ohio General Assembly, has very strict guidelines as to who is permitted to view an execution. State laws vary as to who is allowed to view an execution and unless I fit into any of the outlined criteria and received permission from an inmate, it would be nearly impossible.

She then told me that since I seemed so polite and interested and since no one had ever called her before and requested such a thing, she was going to send me the Ohio Revised Code statute along with the list of defendants who were actually scheduled to be executed in the coming year and that I could try to see what I can do. I took the state statute and brought it to Roger. We decided that the best route to take was to contact the defendants themselves and see if they were willing to speak to me and perhaps ask me to be one of their witnesses since they are allowed to choose their witnesses. Usually, the three witnesses consist of one clergy and two attorneys.

Working as a prosecutor for a number of years, Roger knew quite a few of the attorneys who defended death penalty cases so he was willing to make some phone calls for me. I also happened to have one more ace in my hand. It seemed that one of the defendants on the execution list that year was related to Roger by marriage. His name was Christopher Newton, and Roger knew him quite well.

With dozens of letters written to various inmates on each of Ohio's two death rows at the time and making countless phone calls to different attorneys, invitations came to speak with inmates face-to-face leading me down a path to learning everything I could about death row and the execution process.

CHAPTER 2

OHIO'S DEATH ROW

Chillicothe, Ohio- Home to death Row

As of 2020, Ohio's death row houses 140 inmates which reside at the Chillicothe Correctional Institution located in Chillicothe, Ohio (Death Row Populations Figures from NAACP Legal Defense and Educational Fund, Inc. October, 2020). This does not include the one female on Ohio's death row who is housed at Marysville Correctional Institution for women. When I first started this project, Ohio had a death row in Mansfield, Ohio, and one in Youngstown, Ohio. Originally, Ohio's death row was housed in the old Ohio Penitentiary in Columbus, Ohio. Here, inmates were housed on death row from 1885 until 1972. Death row was then moved to the Southern Ohio Correctional Facility in Lucasville, Ohio, where it stayed from 1972 until 1995. It was moved out of Lucasville due to the riots that took place there in 1993. From Lucasville, death row was moved to Mansfield Correctional Institution in Mansfield, Ohio where it stayed until 2005. In 2005, death row was moved to the supermax prison in Youngstown, Ohio, until January 1, 2012. The state of Ohio decided that due to costs and security and the fact that Youngstown's supermax prison was turned over to a private corporation known as Correction Corporation of America, which was the fifth largest private prison system in the nation with seventy-eight facilities, it would be best to move death row to the Chillicothe Correctional Institution located in Chillicothe, Ohio. This location was also closer to the death house still located in Lucasville, Ohio, which would make it easier to transport the inmates to their execution (Alan Johnson, Columbus Dispatch, October 3rd. 2011). After some rioting took place there at that prison, Ohio's Department of Corrections decided to move death row to Mansfield while keeping the death chamber at Lucasville. The state of Ohio then decided to construct a super max institution in Youngstown, Ohio, that would house the worst of the worst offenders as well as death row inmates. However, not everyone was transferred from Mansfield's death row to Youngstown. If an inmate required special medical care or mental health care, they would stay in Mansfield, all others would go to Youngstown. Some of the inmates I spoke to decided to stay in Mansfield because they would still be able to smoke and do other things. Apparently, it seems like it didn't really matter who was one of the worst killers after all. All male death row inmates are currently housed in Chillicothe, Ohio (Ohio Death Penalty Center.org, 01/01/20).

In 2012, the Ohio Department of Corrections decided to privatize the supermax prison in Youngstown. The state turned it over to a for-profit agency to run in order to alleviate some of the costs of taxpayers for housing prisoners. They closed down death row there, as well as the death row in Mansfield. For whatever reason, the state decided to move all of the death row inmates to one of the oldest prisons in the state of Ohio located in Chillicothe while still housing the death house in Lucasville. The day before an execution takes place, the condemned inmate is transferred under strong security all the way to Lucasville by bus to be housed until he is executed. If you are thinking that all of this appears to be unorganized, confusing, and expensive, you are right. It is.

Death row inmates housed in Huntsville, Texas or San Quentin, California, are condemned inmates locked down 23 hours a day with one hour of exercise a day inside of what looks to be a large dog kennel. The inmates are restricted on everything from movement to when they can shower. They are also extremely limited on every aspect of outside life and amenities. Most death row inmates are allowed visitation only during certain times a month, and the majority of those visitations take place through glass windows. There is no contact between them and another person. Their cells are small, usually filthy, and it is very loud. They rarely ever come into contact with another human being unless they are shackled with chains and handcuffed. They live out their days on death row just like this until the day arrives for them to be executed. They are, for all intents and purposes, caged and warehoused like animals waiting to be killed. The general public knows, understands, and accepts this. In fact, even under the most extreme and grueling conditions, most people feel no sympathy towards those inmates whatsoever (deathpenaltyinformationcenter.org, 01/01/20).

There is a very good reason why you won't see Ohio's death row featured on any television show or documentary. This death row is unlike any I have ever seen. In fact, I believe that once people discover for themselves how the condemned inmates are treated on this death row, the general public might just become outraged.

They say that there are two sides to every story and somewhere in between lies the truth. In order to show how death row really is, without bias from others, I decided to deal directly with the inmates on death row myself instead of going through guards, attorneys, or families.

No system is perfect, and flaws will exist in every part of an institution; however, when a visitor, such as myself, can walk into three different death rows on countless occasions and never be asked to keep my handcuff key locked up somewhere, there is a major problem.

A handcuff key in the hands of a prisoner is like gold to them. These keys are universal and fit all handcuffs. I never once tried to sneak this past the guards. It has always been on my key ring with my other, normal keys. In fact, there was only one time, when I was visiting an inmate on Mansfield's death row that I thought I was going to get reprimanded for having it. As I was signing in and emptying my pockets, the guard picked up my keys, looked directly at me and said, "I should have you locked up right now." It was probably my tenth visit to the prison, and I expected to be turned away. I figured it would be a good entry in my notes: number of visits before handcuff key is discovered on my keyring. Instead, the guard said, "Having a Steeler's key in the middle of Brown's country" and tossed them right back to me.

I simply said, "Well, everyone has their faults; maybe one day you will come around." Then I walked right on in and off to death row I went. Mansfield, Youngstown, and

Lucasville prisons have all let me go in with my keys, each time. Chillicothe was the only death row where they made me lock up my keys and other personal property. I have had my keys on me during every execution that I have witnessed. I never let an inmate know I had this on me, and I would hate to imagine what they would do in order to get it from me.

Most of my visits to the prisons in Mansfield, Ohio, and Chillicothe, Ohio, were one-on-one with no direct supervision and no handcuffs on the inmate. The prison located in Mansfield, Ohio, is called Mansfield Correctional Institute. To those who have been sentenced to this prison, it is known as simply MANCI. For those who are not familiar with this prison, it is located next to the old Ohio State Reformatory, which is best known for the film *Shawshank Redemption*. The old prison was shut down, and all prisoners were transferred to the new facility in 1990 (The Ohio State Reformatory Preservation Society). Currently, the old Ohio State Reformatory is used for tours, events, and even overnight stays for those who wish to get the feel of what it was like there when it housed the inmates. Many of those same inmates are still incarcerated in the new facility which can been seen from across the yard. The prison located in Chillicothe, Ohio, is the oldest prison in the state still in use today. It is called the Chillicothe Correctional Institution today but was better known as the Ohio State Penitentiary. Sometimes, we would be able to walk up and down that area of death row with no one close to us at all. These inmates have absolutely nothing to lose. They are going to die. I've heard more than one of my inmates say to me, "If I could just kill one more person, they wouldn't be able to execute me right away since they'd have to try me in court again." That's an eerie thing for someone to say to you when you look around, and you are the only other person in sight.

When you are dealing with criminals having only weeks or days to live, all bets are off. There is no one who can predict what behavior they might exhibit. They sometimes become so desperate that nothing is beyond them if it will extend their life a little longer. Most of them have extended their time on death row for many years as they successfully won their appeals. Their phantom dates with death were meaningless. However, when they get down to the last three or four weeks of their life, they are irrational and desperate. They start thinking that maybe they could save their life by taking mine, at least for another year or two.

I will never forget one specific day that I spent on death row in Mansfield with an inmate by the name of Chris Newton. Chris was always interesting to visit and interview because he welcomed his execution like no one I had ever met before. He could not wait to be executed. He killed his cellmate years before in order to be put on death row. He hated society and hated prison. Just like most of my inmates though, he could kill anyone at any time except for himself.

Inmates on death row do not like the idea of suicide. It is their strange belief that God will forgive them of all of their sins except killing themselves so since they all want to go to Heaven; the death row inmate can't commit suicide. So, after Newton beat his cellmate the death, he smeared the blood all over himself, drank some of it, masturbated on the body, then sat down and ate a pear while he waited for the guards. All of this happened in protective custody within the prison. He never denied any of this and stated he would keep killing until the state executed him. He got what he asked for, and that's when I met him, on death row.

Newton and I sat in a room in Mansfield on death row so I could interview him in private. There were no windows or bars, just a table, cement walls, and a heavy steel door with no opening. We were discussing his up-and-coming execution that was only about five days away. After an hour or so, a case worker walked in on us. Every inmate I ever dealt with on Mansfield's death row hated this particular case worker. All of them told me how he always acted better than anyone else and never treated any of them with respect.

He had given me the run around a few times, but I always dismissed it due to the job stress he faced every day dealing with these guys.

When this caseworker walked in and saw Newton laughing with chewing tobacco in his mouth, he looked straight at Newton and said, "Newton, you know damn well I could write you up right now for that. You know you're not allowed to have chew in here."

Chris stopped laughing and the look that came over his face was enough to frighten Satan. Chris looked right at the caseworker and said, "Yeah, well I've wanted to kill you since the day I got here. In fact, the only reason I haven't killed you is because if I did, then they would push my date back, and I'm ready to die; so help me, if you don't get the fuck out of here right now, I'll kill you in a heartbeat."

The caseworker's eyes got wide, and he looked directly at me and said, "He's all yours. Call when you're done." He turned around and walked out, shut and locked the door behind him.

I sat there for a second and looked at Newton who said to me, "So what were we talking about?"

I said the only thing that came to mind, "You were talking about killing him, not me!"

He just laughed and said, "Oh him, he's just a little prick that everyone hates. I like you."

Then we went back to talking about his up-and-coming execution, and he told me who else he would like to kill if he had the time before being executed. This was my first lesson in dealing with so many sociopaths on death row. Never get too complacent and never underestimate their willingness and ability to kill.

It was also the time I discovered that the norms and values of society do not exist on death row. They say that prison itself is a whole different society, while death row is an entirely different society within the prison. It's been my experience over the years that for the inmates on death row, the only life that has any value on death row is their own. Everyone else's life means nothing to them. Whether or not they felt this way before arriving on death row I do not know, but I do know that by the time the inmates are ready to leave this is how they feel.

Now that all of the condemned inmates are housed on one death row in Chillicothe, it is much easier to schedule my visits. The downside is that the drive is much further than it was when I drove to Mansfield, but it's about the same drive time as when I used to drive to Youngstown to see those inmates. While the inmates hate the age of the prison and how outdated it is for them, they all seem to love the freedom they get now while being on death row. The state opened the prison in 1966 to house maximum level offenders. Prior to that, the prison was used as a military camp as well as a federal prison (Ohio Department of Rehabilitation and Corrections, 2012). There is no 23 hour a day lockdown, no isolation from others, and very little restrictions on visitations. Now they get to enjoy amenities that most inmates in general population don't even get to enjoy! (Ohio Department of Rehabilitation and Corrections, 2012).

Imagine having your own color television with TV antennas, hand-held video games, mp3 players and access to download music, and typewriters. Imagine not having to share your cell with another inmate. The inmates on death row in Chillicothe have privacy and freedom to move about and visit other inmates. They have painting supplies that include canvases, oil paints, and brushes, and other craft materials to make wooden boxes or clocks. They have mail service and can receive, not just letters from the outside world but up to three fully nude pictures a day!

Most of the inmates I have dealt with on death row have raped women and children at some point in their life, yet they are still allowed to receive up to three nude pictures a day in the mail, as long as none of the pictures contain any penetration. (You will not find these rules in any of the published handbooks, this is something that is just well known to those on death row and to those of us who have seen it first-hand). It seems ironic that rapists can receive nudity but nothing as graphic such as penetration. This line in the sand that the Department of Corrections has drawn seems fruitless to me. Even more surprising than permission to receive these nude pictures are the number of women who are willing to send them to these inmates.

These same inmates are also allowed to receive money from the outside through J Pay money orders. They can also email people on the outside, order shoes, clothes, and just about anything else through a specific site or have people order for them to be delivered to them in prison. There are literally hundreds of different food items that can be ordered and delivered to the inmates in a food box: soups, meat, candy, chips, anything. All of this and more can be ordered and shipped to Ohio's death row. Of course, each time you order goods or send a money order to an inmate, the site charges a fee. I guess that's one way to profit off an inmate and justify it all at the same time ("Send Packages to Inmates Incarcerated in Correctional Facilities").

Just a couple of years ago there was an inmate scheduled to die on this death row by the name of Ron Post. On a last-minute stay, the governor decided to commute his sentence to life without parole based on issues dealing with his representation at trial. Mr. Post, who weighed in excess of 400 pounds, was transported to general population and soon after died from a massive heart attack. The sad reality is that they could not find his veins in order to execute him, and they were not sure how the drugs would work on such an obese person. In typical political fashion, the governor stated reasons for his commuting of the sentence to life as having to do with his counsel and not the truth being they didn't know what to do with him. All along the real question should have been, why did the Department of Corrections allow him to become so obese to begin with? Well, I guess when you, as an inmate, can order whatever food you want to go along with whatever else the prison serves you every day, and you decide not to be active but instead sit around and play video games all day, then things like this are bound to happen (Mueller).

Other states such as California and Louisiana have come under fire in recent years due to the conditions of their death rows: lockdown for 23 hours a day, no proper ventilation, no recreational activities, poor food, and denial of adequate health and mental health care. Conditions so horrible in fact that more death row inmates on San Quentin's death row in California have committed suicide than have been executed in the past 30+ years. Article 3 of the Equality and Human Rights Commission protects from torture and inhuman or degrading treatment or punishment ("Article 3: Freedom from Torture and Inhuman or Degrading Treatment").

In May 2014, Ohio's death row population also filed complaints to the state capital. What were the complaints alleged by Ohio's worst of the worst? Birds and bird droppings in their cells and lack of hot water in their cells. Ohio's 138 death row inmates only requested screens for their cell windows and more hot water to go with their private cells. There seems to be a lot of discrepancy between states when it comes to the treatment of those on death row (Welsh-Higgins).

While arguments can be made on both sides as to whether inmates are treated too well in Ohio or too badly in other states, the fact remains that we are just warehousing these individuals until the final legal proceeding takes place, which is their execution. It is my personal belief that offering any type of rehabilitation programs to inmates who are condemned to die makes no sense. They are not there to be rehabilitated like other offenders. They are there to await their pending execution.

The conditions of the inmates' cells, food, ventilation, and recreation time could all be considered subjective as determined by those in charge. The blatant and obvious discrepancies between Ohio's death row and other states' death rows strikes me as very odd. One would think that in this country and in this day and age we would have some type of universal protocol for housing and executing inmates for the thirty-two states that utilize the death penalty. If we have federal laws for all fifty states that mandate how we must care for our sick, our elderly, and our children, then shouldn't every state be on the same page when it comes to the ultimate punishment of taking another person's life? Unfortunately, just as no two executions are ever the same, no two states can agree on the proper protocol for death row or the method of execution to be used.

CHAPTER 3

THE DEATH PENALTY IN THE UNITED STATES TODAY

According to the Death Penalty Resources website (deathpenaltyinformationcenter.org, 2021) there are approximately 2,500 inmates on death row in the United States as of April 2021. To date, we have thirty-five states in this country that can put people to death. The United States government as well as the United States military can also execute people in this country. New Mexico, Connecticut, and Maryland have abolished the death penalty in their states, but the laws enacted to abolish it were not made retroactive. This means that they still have inmates on death row awaiting execution, but no one else can be placed on death row in those states.

There are various execution methods still utilized here in the United States.

Gas Chamber
The gas chamber, which is only used in three states today - Arizona, Missouri, and Wyoming - has been used eleven times since 1976. While an effective way to an end one's life, this method is still considered barbaric by most standards. The actual cause of death in the gas chamber is hypoxia,

which occurs when oxygen to the brain is cut off. Sodium cyanide crystals are combined with sulfuric acid in a bucket underneath the chair where the inmate is strapped down. The chemical reaction releases hydrogen cyanide gas which rises up. He either inhales the noxious gases or holds his breath until he nearly passes out, forcing him to breathe in the poisonous gas. The inmate's skin turns purple; his eyes usually pop out; he convulses and seizes during the entire time the poisonous gas is being inhaled. It is estimated that it takes approximately twenty minutes for the inmate to die. Even after the inmate is dead, the body must remain in the chamber for nearly an hour in order for the exhaust fans to remove the poisonous gases. The body must then be sprayed down with ammonia to neutralize the cyanide residue left on the body before the dead inmate can be removed ("Description of Each Execution Method").

Gallows

Better known as hanging, gallows can still be used to execute an individual in the states of Delaware, New Hampshire, and Washington. Three people have been put to death by this method since 1976. Unlike other methods of execution, this administration of death requires some calculation in order to be properly done. The inmate's exact height and weight must be taken to calculate the distance of the drop required when the trapdoor is released. The rope must be boiled for a certain length of time to allow for the knot to be placed correctly on the side of the person's neck so that it will ensure proper breakage of the spinal cord once they are dropped. If done properly the inmate's neck snaps, creating almost instantaneous death as the lifeless body rotates and hangs there. However, this does not usually occur. If the proper measurements are not taken, if the rope is not sufficiently prepared, and if the gallows do not provide the necessary drop length, then one of two things will most certainly occur. Either the body will drop too far with such force that the entire head separates from the rest of the body resulting in decapitation, or most likely, the drop is not far enough for the weight of the inmate which results in the person hanging there completely alive but strangling to death. During this slow death, the body's natural defense mechanisms kick in, and they struggle to survive while slowly being choked to death ("Description of Each Execution Method").

Firing Squad
The firing squad is still used in two states: Oklahoma and Utah. Three people have met their fate this way since 1976 with the last one being in 1996 in Utah. Oklahoma only permits this method if both electrocution and lethal injection are ever ruled to be unconstitutional. Utah allows this method only if the inmate was placed on death row prior to lethal injection being made the primary method of execution and the inmate chooses to be executed in this manner. If the inmate refuses to choose, then lethal injection will be the method ("Description of Each Execution Method").

More recently, other states have decided to bring the matter of utilizing the firing squad up as their preferred method of execution instead of lethal injection due to the vast number of cases under legal review for botched executions. Many drug companies have refused to supply the lethal injection drugs to prisons. States are forced to constantly try different drugs to put their inmates to death. Often these drugs have never been tested for this purpose, and no one really knows what the outcome will be. Opponents argue that this violates the eighth amendment regarding cruel and unusual punishment (Death Penalty Information Center, 2021).For a firing squad execution, the inmate is strapped to a wooden chair surrounded by bags of sand or lead. A doctor pinpoints the exact location of the heart and places a target over it. A hood is placed over the inmate's head. Approximately twenty feet away, behind a concealed cover, five marksmen await the word to fire their 30 caliber rifles directly at the target causing the heart to explode instantly. Four of the five marksmen have live rounds, and one person has a blank bullet. No one knows who is shooting the blank, unloaded bullet. If done properly death is almost instantaneous, which is why other states are considering switching to this method of execution ("Description of Each Execution Method").

Electric Chair

The State of New York built the first electric chair in 1888 and executed the first inmate in 1890. Soon after, most states abandoned hanging and went to electrocution as their means of executing their inmates. The electric chair was still the sole method of execution in the state of Nebraska until 2008 when it was ruled unconstitutional by the Supreme Court (Death Penalty Information Center, 2021).

There are currently eight states that still use the electric chair, with Nebraska being the last state to switch over to the lethal injection method as its primary method in 2008. Tennessee has it written in their laws that they will impose the electric chair on its inmates if lethal injection drugs cannot be obtained for a scheduled execution (Death Penalty Information Center, 2021).

The inmate that is to be put to death by electrocution must first have their head and legs shaved. Once they are strapped into the electric chair, a metal skullcap-shaped electrode is attached to the scalp on top of a sponge that has been soaked in a saline solution. Another electrode is attached to the inmate's shaved leg using a conductive jelly. The inmate's face is covered due to the simple fact that once the electricity is passed through a body, it is common for the eyeballs to pop out of the skull. The inmate also often urinates, defecates, and vomits blood once the nearly 2,000 volts surge through their body for thirty second intervals, which is repeated until they are pronounced dead. Since the body is hot enough to blister someone who touches it, the body must cool for a period of time before being removed from the chair. In most cases, all internal organs appear to be cooked on the inside ("Description of Each Execution Method").

Lethal Injection

In 1976, when the United States Supreme Court re-instituted the death penalty, the main method that was used to carry out executions was electrocution. Now however, lethal injection has taken over as the predominant method to use in every state that has the death penalty. Since 1976, there have been approximately 1,214 people executed by lethal injection compared to only 158 who met their death through electrocution. I will explain the method of lethal injection in greater detail in a later chapter (Death Penalty Information Center, 2021).

CHAPTER 4

THE INMATE

People ask me all of the time about the inmates on death row. Are they scary? What do they look like? Are you ever afraid of them? While condemned inmates do come in all shapes, sizes, and colors, the best way that I can describe them would be "dangerously normal!" Some look like your next-door neighbor while others look like they could be college students. It's very rare that an inmate will have "killer" tattooed on their forehead to let you know, with the exception of Stephen Hugueley from Tennessee's death row. More about him later on though.

Most of the time when I sit with these individuals, I have to keep reminding myself who they really are. I have always been treated with the utmost respect from every inmate I have interviewed on death row. When they write me letters, they tend to be very concerned for my well-being and always ask how my book is coming along. They have all appeared to me well-groomed, clean-shaven, and very polite. Most tend to get emotional at some point during our conversations whether it is about past relationships or missing family members. Each time I sat down with Anthony Sowell, for example, who is currently awaiting his execution for raping, murdering, dismembering, and hiding the bodies of eleven females in his home and around his property, he always broke down in tears when his mother was brought up in the conversation.

As someone who holds a doctorate in psychology and not a licensed psychologist, I know how to respond to situations when people, faced with their past, exhibit emotional pain. But in fact, one doesn't need to be a psychologist to offer words of comfort to those experiencing emotional pain and anguish. A simple "I'm sorry for your pain" or "Is there anything I can do to help?" is sufficient for the typical individual. It lets them know that you are there for them; and that, while you may not understand their pain, you are sympathetic to them. However, when a person as evil as Anthony Sowell, sits down with you, eating and drinking freely, and begins to cry, you learn quickly that there is never a typical response to offer a condemned inmate.

It was very difficult for me to maintain any sort of professionalism during my visits with Sowell who is so cold and calculated that he abducted eleven women from the streets of Cleveland, Ohio, and raped, murdered, dismembered, and hid their bodies in his home and then went about his daily routine as if nothing was ever wrong. During our visits, he not only admitted all of his crimes to me, he never once showed remorse for any of his victims. He wanted me to find out why he became the monster he is today. Yet as soon as I would bring up his childhood and his mother, the tears would flow. It would take all I had to be able to sit across from him, watch him cry and not express what was really going through my mind. I kept him talking in order for him to tell me everything he could and reminded myself from time to time that regardless of how I felt, I was still in their house, and I was still an outsider. He was still a serial killer who loved the attention and was still very capable of killing again.

Anthony Sowell always had to feel in complete control of each interview, but he still treated me with respect. He would ask how my drive down was and wanted to make sure that

I got enough to eat while I was visiting with him. The only reason why I stopped talking to Sowell was a disagreement we had over his artwork. He wanted me to purchase his artwork and to pay him for his story. He actually wanted me to write a book specifically about him, and he wanted to control everything from what was going to be included in the book to when I would get specific information from him. He also became very jealous whenever I talked to other inmates. He thought that there was no other person I needed to speak with since he was the most notorious serial killer in the state of Ohio. When he discovered that I was no longer interested in his story and I wasn't going to buy his artwork, he became upset. He decided to give a painting to someone else even though, according to him, he painted it especially for me. He also said he didn't want to talk to me anymore.

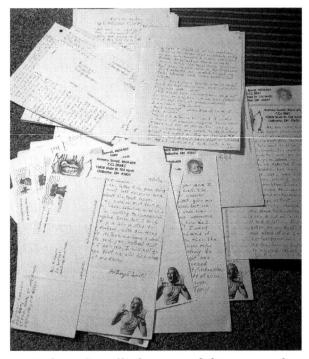

Anthony Sowell's letters with his personal stationary from death row

The letters that Sowell writes are written on his very own stationary which he has printed up and sent to him on death row. As you can see in one of his letters included here, he seems to still be fascinated with terrifying women, much like he did when he killed eleven of them in Cleveland.

I find it fascinating, from a psychological standpoint, that I still receive letters from inmates that I have never met on death row who heard that I am a stand-up guy. They tell me I shouldn't pay any attention to Sowell and, things like, "We would like to talk to you" and "Sowell is just greedy and wants the attention." They will also tell me they are on my side. It feels like I am dealing with seventh graders competing to be my friend instead of inmates on death row.

Of course, not all inmates are like Anthony Sowell. Some are very nondescript. Some have very little to say as they are just waiting until their time to check out. Some are self-educated, and some, like James Filiaggi, were college educated before prison.

Each death row inmate is unique in their own special way, and James Filiaggi was no exception. He was very willing to do whatever he could to educate others about death row and keep others from ever ending up there. On death row for hunting down his ex-wife, chasing her into a neighbor's house, finding her in a closet, and shooting her execution-style, he never once denied his crime or showed remorse for it either.

James turned his attention towards people on the outside and tried to show them his humanity. This seemed to work very well because following his execution there was a huge wake and funeral for him, attended by a couple of hundred people (Lorain Journal, April 27, 2007). For some reason he was able to pull at people's emotional strings. To this day, I still hear people talk about him in Lorain, Ohio. Nothing bad is ever really said about him. Even his attorney, who went on to become a Common Pleas Court Judge, attended his funeral.

What I found particularly unsettling about James was his uncanny ability to impress so many people with his positive attitude, yet I could still see the hatred in his eyes and hear it in his voice when he spoke about society in general. He could turn on a dime emotionally. During our interviews, he would go from being all right and very upbeat about his up-and-coming execution, then the next minute he would be filled with rage. During one of his rages, he told the Clemency Board to kiss his ass and that he was not going to beg anyone for his own life. He would agree that killing someone is wrong, but then he also believed that it was wrong to execute him. He always talked very emotionally about his two daughters and how much he loved and missed them. He said he would do anything to have them close to him again, but he never said that he was sorry for killing their mother.

One of the reasons that I liked interviewing James so much was because he asked me just as many questions as I asked him. He was very interested in learning more about the outside just as I was interested in learning more about the inside. When he found out that I had a son, he sent weekly packages to my PO Box addressed to my then seven-year-old son. They contained kid's magazines, school-type quizzes for math and reading, lots of comics, and usually chewing gum. He always told my son to stay in school and out of trouble and to keep learning. Of course, I never allowed my son to have the gum or even to open anything that James sent, but I did give my son a lot of the educational materials and comics.

In addition to my son, James also sent my wife stuff, particularly recipes. Whenever I interviewed him, he asked me if my wife had tried out any of the recipes that he had sent. One day when James was in a joking mood, I explained to him that my wife's cooking was nothing to brag about. In fact, her cooking and I usually never agreed with each other. I told him that her cooking was so awful that if he wanted to trade places with me, he could eat her cooking and I would take the needle for him. He never sent another recipe.

This is how I treated all of the guys I came into contact with on death row. I treated them just like I would anyone else. This is why I believe that so many of them liked me. They knew I would never lie to them, talk down to them, and I would never act like I was better than them. In return they gave me the utmost respect. James was just the type who would try to show that he was capable of having a heart. He made sure to send out dozens of Christmas cards every year, and he kept a lot of people close to him all the way through to the end.

Now if you are thinking that sharing anything with my son from death row was completely wrong, I already know. I just never realized how wrong I was until after his execution. Following James's execution, I closed his case file just like I do with all of the others after they die. It wasn't until about two or three weeks later that I realized I may have made a big mistake.

My son came up to me one day and asked if I had gotten anything in the mail lately from Jimmy. I said, "Jimmy? Who's Jimmy?"

That's when he said, "You know, your friend on death row. I haven't gotten a package in a while."

Now you would think at this point I would have remembered I was dealing with a child and not an adult; however, I was clearly not thinking at all when I replied instantly, "Oh, James? You won't be getting any more packages from him. He's dead." The look in his eyes and the sound of his voice told me right then that I had made a horrible decision. It was a mistake I would never make again.

James Filiaggi was one of those rare inmates on death row who never seemed to become hardened like all the others and while he never showed any real remorse for his crimes, he also never talked about hurting anyone else. The same cannot be said about any of the others I have dealt with over the years. In fact, most of my inmates seemed to metastasize hatred like cancer metastasizes, the longer they are kept alive. It just keeps growing and spreading until they eventually die. Stephen Hugueley is the perfect example of one such inmate.

Stephen Hugueley, my only death row inmate who is awaiting his execution on Tennessee's death row, looks like a killer, sounds like a killer, and still acts like a killer. He has no regrets, no remorse, and no one is safe around him. He once told me, "If I like you, you're my best friend. If I don't like you, I have to kill you."

Stephen has been featured on MSNBC's Lock-Up (Lockup Raw). He was originally given a life sentence for shooting his own mother fifteen times and dumping her over a bridge before going out on a date. He told me that it was all due to the anger that had built up inside of him over the years because of his parents' divorce. He stated that he told his mom one day that he was going to go stay with his dad in Michigan. That's when she turned to him and told him matter-of-factly that his dad was dead; he had killed himself, and she just never got around to telling him. He never forgave her for that, and one day he just snapped.

While talking to a girl on the phone, his mother asked him if he was talking to "another one of those little whores." He said to the girl on the other end, "I'm fixing to kill my mom. I'll pick you up a little later." That's when he shot his mother fifteen times with a rifle, put her in the trunk of his car, drove to a nearby bridge, and threw her over, then proceeded to go on his date. Once in prison, he decided that he wanted the state of Tennessee to execute him; but since he only received a life sentence for killing his mother, he knew he would have to kill again. He said he would kill until eventually the state would give him the death penalty so he could die by what he considered "suicide by state." He killed another inmate because of a debt owed to him and ended up getting another life sentence for that murder as well. He told me the reason he killed that inmate was because he talked down to him and never intended to pay his debt. He later killed his prison counselor, which eventually got him the death sentence he had been asking for. Hugueley admitted to stabbing his counselor nearly sixty times with a homemade shank.

He told me several times that he has no remorse for any of his murders. He also stated that if anyone ever says that they feel remorse for actually murdering someone then they are lying. Hugueley never denied any of the killings and told me he never thought much about them afterwards. He did tell me once, however, that the only reason they have him in prison for these three murders is because "They never got me for the others." He claims to have killed others but would not go into detail with me on any of those.

Like most killers on death row though, Hugueley loves the attention. In fact, he craves attention. While he may sound very ignorant when he is speaks, Stephen Hugueley knows exactly what he wants while he is still alive. He is extremely organized and methodical when it comes to gaining the attention that he feels he deserves. He wanted his own Stephen Hugueley website to attract people to him and his crimes. He wrote me letters to explain everything that he wanted included on the website. The letters were so thick and so many pages long, literally hundreds of pages at a time, that I had to get them bound. He expressed his anger in some of his letters because I didn't write him back fast enough. His writings included rants, Bible verses, pictures of himself, lists of reporters he had spoken to, and more. He wrote what he called "teachings" to be posted while at the same time told me that he no longer accepted the Bible, Christ, or anything else to do with religion. He just wanted people to see how he used to be. He really wanted people to fear him and to never forget him, just like most killers do.

Hugueley loved to be in control. He wanted complete say in the interviews, on who should be allowed to talk to him, and what should be listed on the website. He even went so far as to send me a handwritten limited power of attorney (see next page) that allowed me total say on how I used what he sent me and giving me complete say in what media outlets could speak to him. He also listed the various media outlets and reporters that I could notify after I interviewed him to have them write about his life. (See complete list on next page.) He was careful about the pictures of him to be posted. He sent me photographs of himself as a baby, young boy, teenager, and finally as an inmate. The pictures show that he did not enter into prison looking like a deranged killer; however, there is no mistaking that is what Stephen Hugueley is today, a cold, calculated, brutal murderer, one who I believe would kill again if he had the chance. The last time I communicated with Stephen via letter, he informed me that the Department of Corrections would not allow him to have access to any visitors face-to-face. It had to be done over the phone or video. They could not trust him enough, and they were afraid he would harm others. Since I was not able to keep up with Stephen's controlling visitation and letter writing schedule, we eventually stopped talking altogether. Knowing him the way I do though, I'm sure if Stephen ever gets to read this book, he will be pleased that he was included in it.

Some inmates that I have spoken to over the years seem to only exist behind the walls of prison. Not all are like Stephen Hugueley or Anthony Sowell. Not everyone wants to be recognized as a mass murderer or serial killer. In fact, I had never actually heard of one particular inmate who wrote to me out of nowhere one day. Yet, I can honestly say that he is the most sadistic human being I have ever sat down with in my entire life. His name is William Sapp.

William first contacted me by letter about a year or so ago. No ordinary letter, it was decorated on the back with a

I Stephen Lynn Hugueley do hereby give Bill Kimberlin the authority to speak to the media about his correspondence with me and the information that I have given him to post on various free websites; Complete power of Attorney shall remain in the hands of my daughter.

Stephen Lynn Hugueley
Stephen Lynn Hugueley #218195
M.C.C.X. / 26-D
P.O. Box 2000
Wartburg, TN 37887

I hereby certify that the afore "Limited Power of Attorney was written and signed by me on this the 7th day of June, 2009.

Stephen Lynn Hugueley

*Steven Hugueley's letter granting me rights to all of his property and art (see full resolution letters and forms at **wbp.bz/wmdgallery**)*

William Sapp and Kimberlin on Ohio's death row

beautifully drawn, full-color Papa Smurf in perfect detail. Across the top of the envelope he wrote, "Have a Smurfic Day Bill." I had no idea who William Sapp was; but judging by his envelope, I assumed that he was going to be a real character. His letter was very well written and almost overly polite. He stated that he had gotten my name from others on death row. He had planned to write me sooner; but because I had just witnessed the execution of his friend the month before, he thought it would have been in poor taste to approach me during that time. He also apologized for the way that Sowell went back on his word to me and told me to not ever worry about him going back on his word. Ever.

He explained to me that he did artwork and was willing to let me interview him as well as witness his execution if I was interested. All that he asked was for some type of compensation for the art supplies that he would be using if I decided that I did want some of his artwork. I decided to write him back, and I told him that I may be interested in learning more from him and wanted him to tell me a little more about himself. In less than a week, I received the second of many more letters to come. This envelope was also very nicely decorated with an eagle on it with the word "freedom" written under the claws of the eagle. Above the eagle was the phrase, "Who knows if life be not death, and death be not life?" This letter piqued my curiosity about Sapp. In this letter, he explained that since I had a good reputation on death row and since I was interested in him, he would put me on his visitation list. He trusted that I would not burn him on anything since I told him in my last letter that I would not be giving him anything towards art supplies or anything else until I was given the artwork first. While reluctant to do so at first, he finally agreed that he would do that.

Nothing in prison is ever free. Nothing! For inmates to send me their paintings, drawings, wooden crafts, personal pictures, and just about anything else that I ask for, without me sending them a single dime, says a great deal about how they perceive me. I have sent money for art supplies and even food boxes to a select group of inmates that I have dealt with over the years, but I never send them anything upfront. I find it psychologically fascinating that hardened death row murderers who trust no one in their lives, trust that I will not burn them by taking their works of art, selling them on the outside, and leaving them with nothing. They pay for the canvasses, paints, brushes, and shipping. They send me whatever they have and then patiently wait to hear what I have to say about their work ("Send Packages to Inmates Incarcerated in Correctional Facilities").).

What I found fascinating about William Sapp was the fact that his letters were so cordial and polite. Every letter began the same way and continues to this day, "Greetings and salutations, I hope this letter found you in the best of health and spirits." While most of the inmates begin their letters with something positive, Sapp always seemed to be genuine. He never really asked me to provide him with much of anything, and he always apologizes in his letters if he uses foul language or feels that he may have offended me. It is psychologically baffling that murderers worry about offending me with their use of language yet never worry about the human lives they have taken in such horrific ways.

After receiving numerous letters from William in which he tells me about how evil he is and how he tried several times to set his biological mother on fire by the age of nine, he invited me down to see him if, in his own words, "I can handle it." He stated that he offered interviews to other people in the past, but they were so disgusted with his lust for raping and killing that they decided not to visit him. He felt that since I was very familiar with death row and that I had seen more than anyone else, he thought I could be the one to hear his story. I decided to set up a visit with him.

Just before going to see William, I received another letter from him in which he began to reveal his true side. It was decorated with a full-color drawing of Mickey Mouse. On the top of the envelope he wrote, "Your life becomes what you think." In the letter, he wrote that he couldn't wait to finally sit down with me and get this adventure going. He had no regrets for any of the killings and rapes that he committed over the years. He awaits the chance to get off of death row and back into the world, "be it legally or illegally" because he says he is "far from being done." He wrote that he truly missed being able to kill, rape, and torture and "It's in my blood, I was born to do this, I enjoy doing this, I love it, and I'm great at it." He proceeded to explain that he loves sex, and it doesn't matter to him if it is with man, woman, child, or animal. "If a girl is 10 years old or older, I'll fuck her. Pussy is pussy, and I'm not going to ID them." He would not have a girl tell him no; and if he needed to take her brutally, which almost always was the case, then so be it. He told me that he grew up thinking this way starting with his "real mother." He was raped by his biological mother as well as his two stepsisters but insists that he really "got into it." He even went so far as to have his stepmom's name, Patricia, tattooed on his upper arm. He also said that while he had sex with his family, he didn't rape anyone until the age of 14 or 15, and that was his stepsister's best friend.

Aside from this letter being so graphic, William also asked me a lot of questions about myself. When I write my guys on death row and ask them questions, I also let them know that they can ask me anything as well. This builds up the trust that is so crucial in my opinion which allows them to open up their world to me. Some of his questions were: Are you staying busy teaching this semester? What is the difference between abnormal psychology, social psychology, and regular psychology? What is your favorite time of year? What is your favorite animal to hunt? He wrote that Halloween was his favorite holiday and "My favorite thing to hunt is human beings." After receiving this letter, how could I not sit down face-to-face with him and interview him in person?

My first visit with William caught us both off guard a little. The first thing he said to me was, "I was expecting someone a lot older and more frail." He was not expecting someone my size, which is 6'4" and about 250 pounds. My first thought was, "I wonder if he was expecting someone older and smaller so he could try to kill them?"

Usually when I visit inmates on death row the guards have really no interest. However, when I visited Sapp, they seemed to be very interested in what he might say to me, since no one really ever visits him, and he is so strange. One guard asked me flat out if I was going to find out how many people he actually killed. I told him I had no idea what I was going to find out, and I asked him why he wanted to know. He told me that law enforcement and federal officials suspected Sapp of committing seventy murders, but they could never prove it. While that caught me off guard a little, I politely told him that I would see what he had to say, and I left it at that.

When I visit the inmates alone, they have no handcuffs on. I am also allowed to get up and freely move around and purchase items out of the vending machines for us both to eat and drink. There is a microwave next to the vending machines that can be used to cook any of the frozen food items purchased there. A lot of the guys usually go for the sweet stuff, and Mountain Dew is usually their drink of choice. Some actually get excited for their interviews because of what they get to eat the entire time I'm talking with them. At the end of the cell block or pod is an old desk where a guard sits. I guess he's there to keep an eye on the inmate although he is so far down from us that if anything ever did happen, I'm sure I would be dead before he got to us. This section of death row is used only for visitations, but the cells and the pod are set up just as if they are still housing inmates. At the opposite end of the block a large flat screen television is mounted with benches in front of it so people can sit and watch TV during their visit. The entire block always seems to be extremely clean and quiet. The only disruption that has ever occurred during my countless visits here are the occasional fly-bys of birds that get inside and just fly around.

When Sapp and I sat down alone at a little round table fastened to the floor with attached seats, we made small talk at first. Right away, I noticed that he has no emotional affect about him, no excitability or anything. Most death row inmates welcome some type of human interaction from the outside and show it through gestures and voice. Not Sapp. He was just matter-of-fact about everything. He was well-groomed, soft-spoken, and very polite. He would not eat unless I ate with him, and he would not drink anything unless I got myself something to drink as well. He was almost guarded with his responses to my questions about being on the inside for the last thirteen years. When I asked him what he missed the most, he calmly replied, "Killing and Zero bars!" He went on to say that he really enjoyed killing people and raping them but that he also missed eating Zero candy bars. He remembered enjoying them as a kid and that they soothed him sometimes after doing "certain things." He said he hadn't had one of those candy bars since getting locked up. I knew I had seen those exact candy bars in the vending machine on other visits so I went to check. Luckily, they were in stock, so I bought two of them and laid them down in front of him at our table. That was the first sign of emotion that I saw from William. I could see him relax his facial muscles, and he asked me in an excited voice, "Where did you find these at?"

I replied lightly, in a joking way, "That's an awful dumb question coming from a guy like you. It's not like I ran to the store to buy them for you."

He laughed and shoved one of the candy bars down his pants. He said he would save that one for later. I asked him if he was worried that they might catch him with it when they take him back to his cell block after our visit to which he informed me that the guards never search them anymore, either before or after visits.

I decided that since he was much more relaxed now, I would ask him about his killings. I told him that the guards informed me that he was good for close to seventy murders and that I wanted to know if this was true or not. He looked me dead in the eyes and said, "No, that is not true at all. When a person kills another human being be it intentional or not, they never forget it. You are going to come across guys who say they killed this many or that many just to get the publicity; but then all of a sudden, they can't remember how or where they supposedly did it. They are fucking liars then. You never forget a murder even if you try to. I've killed fifty people. I can prove fifty people, not one single more, so they don't know what the hell they're talking about when they say I did seventy."

He then went on to explain that he tried to save at least one thing from every one of his victims. Sometimes it was a ring, other times it was the entire finger. Sometimes it was a necklace, other times it was a nipple. He also described himself as a "cleaner." When he disposed of a body, he made sure to clean everything completely to prevent getting caught. He also tried to hide and bury them in locations that were difficult to get to near railroad tracks or close to any dumping grounds that would help mask the scent of the body as it decomposed. William went on to explain that he enjoyed having sex with the victims after he killed them. In fact, he told me he thought it was odd that more guys wouldn't admit to having sex with the dead bodies after they killed their victims.

During the entire time he was explaining everything to me, he continued to eat his food and drink his Mountain Dew as though this was normal behavior. He explained that he was not capable of loving anyone in life and that he regretted not killing his wife and kids when he could. He said he hadn't seen them since being put on death row and has no desire to see them. I asked him what he would say to his kids, now adolescents, if he did see them. He thought for a second then simply stated, "I wouldn't say anything. In fact, if I could, I would still kill them right now." He then went back to eating.

William and I talked a lot on that first visit and over the course of the last year or so. My goal was to get as many names and locations of victims from him as possible to hopefully provide some sort of closure to families who had lost a loved one. William was just happy to have found someone who could put up with him without judging him or feeling disgusted towards him. He was willing to give up what he felt was the ultimate control over people by giving me information, not out of remorse but to make a "great story." This goes to show that most serial killers, if not all, still want their fifteen minutes of fame. Their worst fear isn't being put to death; their worst fear is to be forgotten by society while they are still alive.

Sadly though, the discovery of bodies, closure for many victims' families, and the closing of the cold cases was not to be. He provided me with three different detailed maps that outlined the exact locations of three different bodies and a detailed description of one of the victims and what she was wearing when William buried her. However, no search has ever been made to find them. Why? That is a question that I keep asking myself over and over. I met with agents from the Federal Bureau of Investigation to discuss the cases and turned over the maps and descriptions. I got answers to the questions they instructed me to ask William Sapp. One FBI agent told me that due to egos and politics, no one was willing to move on the information. They firmly believed that Sapp killed people in Ohio and Florida, yet the local departments in the towns on the maps do not want to stir up cases. To make matters worse, Sapp's attorneys were somehow notified that he was talking to me and giving me information so now our communication has nearly been cut off.

Here is a guy sentenced to die in Ohio's execution chamber who is willing to give me the locations of numerous bodies and to let me help ease the pain of so many families out there from Ohio to Florida; but due to egos, attorneys, and politics, this won't happen. I'm sure the family members out there who have maybe wondered for years if they will ever know what happened to their daughter, sister, mother, or aunt will completely understand.

Kimberlin and Sapp eating together on death row during an interview.

In the last letter that I received from William, he assured me that he was a man of his word and that before he was executed, he would give me everything I wanted. He also informed me that mail from me hasn't always been delivered to him and that the letters he has sent to me have not always made it out of the prison. I still hope one day I will be able to locate the victims he says are out there and bring some peace to the families who are left wondering. If that happens, then I can honestly say that every minute I spent dealing with this "Satan in Disguise" will have been worth it. Until then though, I will keep asking why. Why not just look and see if they are really there? What's the worst that can happen? If nothing is found, then tell me and everyone else that you told me so and that I don't know what I'm talking about. If the FBI is willing to bust through concrete and tear down buildings just to look for the body of Jimmy Hoffa, then why not dig in a few wooded areas in Ohio and Florida? Is it because the victims were prostitutes? Is it because if you do find something then your egos will be bruised? Maybe Sapp is leading me on a wild goose chase, spinning lies, but just maybe he is telling the truth.

There was only one person Sapp admitted to actually liking in prison. That person was Christopher Newton. Sapp once told me that the only reason he and Chris got along so well was because no other people on the face of this earth were as sick and twisted as they were.

Chris Newton was a sick individual. No one could argue with that. He was also very dangerous. He is the only person on death row that I have come into contact with who actually couldn't wait to be executed. Sapp and Newton would trade stories back-and-forth about how they would love to get out and rape again. In fact, the day before Newton's execution, he was really hoping to at least get under the shirt or inside the pants of his cousin who was there for his last visitation. He told me his plan was to bribe her since she really wanted to be there at his execution. He was going to tell her that if she would let him feel her breasts and play with her vagina really quick when the guards were not looking, then he would let her watch him be executed. I can't say what took place between them the night before his execution when his family got to see him for the last time, but I do know that she was not present during his execution. It was only me, his spiritual advisor, and his attorney when he was put to death.

Newton's execution, which took a little over two hours from start to finish, convinced me that there is no such thing as a botched execution. There is, however, poor planning, lack of training, and ignorant officials who only claim they know what they are doing. The only saving grace with Newton's execution was the fact that he wanted to die! During his preparation, just before his execution he was joking with the execution team and smiling the entire time they were sticking needles in his arms, legs, and neck trying to find a suitable vein. Ohio requires two separate ports of entry for the administration of the lethal injection. Since there are no medical doctors allowed to take part in the execution process, only prison staff and trained EMTs prepare the inmate. Sometimes, it is very difficult to find the veins if the person is obese or has used a lot of intravenous drugs in the past. Knowing Chris Newton, the way I did, he was neither obese nor an IV drug abuser. As I sat quietly observing the individuals who were trying to find the veins on Chris, I couldn't help but notice how a few of them were shaking themselves. Their hands were far from steady which told me that they too were having issues being put in this position of assisting in the killing of another human being.

Once they were able to locate a vein in one of the arms, they started the bag of saline solution to keep that vein from closing back up while locating the second vein. At that point, I could really see the worry on their faces. They tried to find veins by sticking him in the leg, then neck, and up and down the arm. It took so long in fact that the bag of saline solution ran dry. Then came the moment that no one was expecting, Newton had to go to the bathroom! It seems that all of that saline that ran through his veins found its way to his bladder. I will never forget the shock and stunned disbelief on their faces when Newton turned his head to tell the execution team that he had to take "a piss."

At this point, the entire execution process seemed completely surreal, watching members of the execution team look at each other and shrug as if to say "now what?" and then watching the condemned man getting up to be led to the bathroom so he can urinate. This brought all kinds of questions to mind! So many questions in fact that I turned to Newton's state public defender who sat right next to me in the death house, and I said to him, "Listen, I don't think this is going as planned. Don't you think you should be in there saying or doing something?"

He looked at me and said, "You think?"

Now I'm not a lawyer, but I do have one year of law school under my belt. I would think, as an attorney, you would want to defend your client until the very end. Newton's attorney said "All right" and got up and went to see about getting into the same room as his client. A minute or so later he came back and sat back down next to me. I asked him what they said, and he replied, "They just told me to go back to my seat and that everything's under control."

Looking at him reminded me of a young boy who was just told to go sit down by his teacher and to be quiet. It was during this execution that I seriously began to question the entire judicial system as well as the Ohio Department of Corrections.

Newton finished using the restroom and lay back down on the table. They located another vein, and he was finally led over to the deathbed where he was strapped down. When it was time to hook up the lines coming from the execution room to Newton's arms, one guard was shaking so much that another guard had to come over and help him by holding the line steady. Newton's final statement was, "Boy, I could sure go for a bowl of soup and a chicken bone."

I have no idea what that meant. The warden then gave the signal to the executioner to start the drugs. As Newton laid there gasping for air with his chest convulsing and making all types of noises, I began to wonder if what I was doing was worth it. I was led to believe that executing someone by lethal injection was similar to putting an animal down. They just go to sleep. Chris Newton was by no means a nice guy; and thinking about his victims who must have suffered

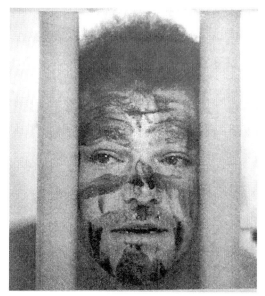

Chris Newton covered in his victim's blood.

Chris newton in a cell moments after murdering his cell mate.

a horrible death, it was difficult to feel any sympathy for Newton. But he was still a human being, and he was being killed right in front of me. I was just a spectator to a completely legal murder.

Not all death row inmates appear completely sinister or evil. Some can be very cheerful when I meet them. One colorful inmate, Miss Frances Anne Spisak, was by far the most psychologically confused inmate I have ever dealt with over the years. Miss Frances Anne was really Frank Spisak. Frank shot five completely innocent people at Cleveland State University. Three of them were killed during his 1982 rampage. Spisak was sent to death row for these deaths and remained there for twenty-eight years until his execution finally took place.

In my opinion what made Spisak psychologically distorted was due in part to the nature of his crimes. Frank Spisak was a self-proclaimed Nazi. Obsessed with Nazi Germany, he wanted to become the next Adolf Hitler. He even dressed the part including the Hitler style mustache and saying "Heil Hitler" throughout his trial. Spisak aspired to become the highest-ranking member of the skinheads and believed that by targeting and killing black and/or Jewish people, he would move up the ranks faster. His entire belief system was based on being a White Anglo Saxon Protestant (WASP). According to Spisak, anyone who wasn't one should be eliminated from society. This included gays, lesbians, transgendered individuals, and anyone else who did not subscribe to this belief.

Fast forward to the years spent on death row. Frank discovered that he was really a woman trapped in a man's body and wanted to become a female. So much so that he tried to get the state of Ohio to pay for his gender reassignment surgery before he was executed. Fortunately for the taxpayers of this state, that didn't happen, but that didn't stop Frank from taking on the persona of a female and changing his name to Frances Anne. This complete transformation is very complex because he went from Frank to Frances and from hater to lover. Frank went from hating transgenders to becoming one. He went from hating African Americans to having sex with them on death row. He went from shunning religion to having not one but two different spiritual advisors on the day of his execution, one of them an African-American minister. During the time I spent talking to Frank (he preferred to be called Frances), he was the most soft-spoken and courteous inmate. He even went so far as to thank me for taking time out of my busy schedule to come to his execution! Less than an hour from death yet, he seemed more concerned about the four-hour drive that I had to make there and back.

In every single letter Spisak wrote to me, he was open and polite. He answered all of my questions and offered to provide any other information I wanted about his life on death row, even if I hadn't asked. The letters were always written in bright pink ink, every letter "i" dotted with a little heart, and he signed them, "love Frances Anne."

He openly admitted to having sex with whomever he could on death row and could always find a spot to do it. Most of the time it was with other inmates; but there were also guards who would have sex with him on occasion as well. This was confirmed by a few other inmates I interviewed who also admitted to doing more than just watching. In fact, Spisak was so open about this behavior that in one of the letters he sent he actually asked if we could not mention his sex life anymore because the guards were "on to us" and had threatened to cut him off sexually which he did not want to happen. He said we could discuss anything else from that point on except sex. Other inmates told me that everyone knew that Frank was into guys, so whenever they felt an urge or a need they went to his cell and would have either oral sex or anal sex, whatever they were in the mood for, with Frank, no questions asked.

I didn't get to spend as much time with Spisak as I did with most of my other inmates. One day I received a letter from the prison with a woman's name on the return address. I actually thought it was from a female death row inmate. I was both shocked and intrigued when I discovered it was really a male inmate. When Spisak first contacted me, he was already close to the end. He never once asked me for anything, no food boxes, no money orders, nothing at all. He asked if I would like to witness his execution, and I told him that I would.

I was the very last person to see him before they took him away to prep him. We talked about his daughter who had come to see him the night before, for the first time since being placed on death row twenty-eight years ago. She was now thirty-two. He was so happy that she came to visit and even took pictures together with her. He shared those pictures of them together with me, as well as an old picture of himself that he wanted people to remember him by.

He told me that he was no longer the monster that killed those people and that he regretted that part of his life. He freely admitted his guilt to me and said he left that monster behind a long time ago. He wanted me to have his pictures to use in any way I saw fit. As we talked, the final order that denied his final appeal for a stay of execution was faxed over. The guards then tapped me on the shoulder and told me it was time. When I got up to leave, Frank shook my hand and asked me if I thought he should die. I asked him what he meant by that, and he said, "As a doctor in psychology and me being bipolar and all, do you think I should be executed today?"

I simply stated that as a I was not comfortable answering that question since I had never had the opportunity to formally diagnose him, and as for my personal opinion, I was not one to judge anyone else. He thanked me once again for my honesty and wished me well. Leaving the death cell to go over to the witnessing room, I felt that Spisak was truly

*Frank Spisak in 1978 that he gave to
me the day of his execution.*

*Spisak with his daughter that he hadn't seen in
nearly 30 years. Day before his execution.*

Spisak having his last meal with his daughter.

remorseful for the crimes that he had committed. Once again, I was wrong.

When Spisak entered the death chamber to be strapped to the execution table, he looked like a deer in headlights. Every inmate is given the opportunity to make a last statement before the sentence of death is carried out, and Spisak was no exception. As he was strapped to the table, he asked the warden to hold up the paper on which he had prepared his last statement so he could read it. It only took a few words for me to realize that Frank Spisak was never remorseful about his crimes. As he lay there strapped to the execution table waiting to die with a cross around his neck, he read his last statement in German, rubbing salt in the wounds of those who survived his vicious attack and were sitting only a few feet away. I could hear the anger and disgust from them. One yelled, "Let me in there. I'll kill him myself."

The others were in shock, appalled that a Neo-Nazi mass murderer would be so bold as to read his last statement in German, not once showing any remorse or apologizing for his actions. When he was finished the warden buttoned his top button signaling to the executioner to begin. Frank looked over to me and waved at me. I never waved back.

Fred Treesh was the last person that I witnessed being executed to date. As of February 1, 2015, the state of Ohio has placed a stay on all executions indefinitely until such time that state officials are able to procure the necessary lethal drugs to use. This will be explained more in the last chapter.

Fred was the type of inmate you could never turn your back on. He seemed almost too nice, too willing to talk, and too eager to get out of his own death sentence. However, I found it easier to interview Fred than the others simply because he made me feel welcomed to death row; he always stood up to greet me. He never spoke negatively about other inmates, other than Anthony Sowell, whom he did not like; and he was always straightforward. I learned a lot from Fred

Fred Treesh on Ohio's death row prior to his execution

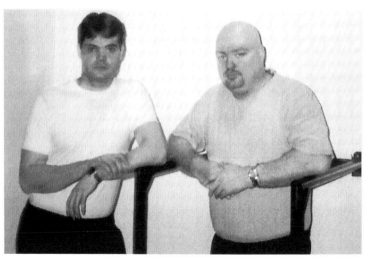

Fred Treesh and his best friend on death row, James Goff

during my time with him. He introduced me to a few other inmates who he said I could trust and who would also take care of me with whatever I needed for my book.

Fred explained to me how being on death row the past eighteen years had changed him. He became more hateful to people on the outside, and he certainly did not like the idea of the victim's family pushing for him to be executed. He admitted to liking the control he had over them simply by appealing the case and making them re-live the events over and over. He blamed everything on his addiction to crack cocaine which he said drove him into the deepest realms of insanity where he would stop at nothing in order to get high. Fred admitted to me that for sixteen out of the eighteen years that he spent on death row he still smoked crack cocaine every chance he got. It was only in the last two years that he quit for good and that was because he made a promise to his mother before she died that he would stop using. Ironically, it was Fred's mother who helped feed his addiction over the years by smuggling in the money for him to buy it.

Fred was completely open with me and explained in great detail just how things worked on death row, especially when it came to getting things. His mother, who was his best friend, visited him often. Each visit she would place a $100 bill inside of a condom. She would then tie the condom up really tight and insert it into her vagina. This would allow her to go undetected through the screening process when she entered the institution. Once inside the prison and the visitation area, she would ask to use the restroom and to be allowed to go to the vending machines. She would first go to the restroom and remove the condom from her vagina that still contained the money. She would then make her way over to the vending machines and purchase a bag of potato chips. She would open the bag of chips while standing at the vending machine and place the condom with the money still inside of it into the bag of chips. She would then go back to sit down and give her son the bag of chips to eat. As Fred would eat the chips, he would also swallow the condom that contained the money she smuggled in. At the end of the day, Fred would then pass the condom out of his body when he had to defecate. When he was finished going to the bathroom, he would pull the condom out of his own feces, tear open the condom, and there he would have a clean $100 bill to buy crack cocaine.

Inmates stated that certain guards brought drugs into the prison and everyone on death row knew who they were. $100 would buy $40 or $50 worth of drugs. Other guards brought in other things such as pornography, but it all came at a high price. Inmates could get just about anything they wanted. All Fred wanted was crack. When his mom was dying, and he knew he could not see her again or be at her funeral, he decided to change his ways of living out the remainder of his sentence on death row. However, while Fred may have changed his ways of living towards the end, he did not change his ways of thinking.

Just days before his execution, the prison allowed Treesh to have three people visit with him one last time. It would be an eight hour visit, and the prison would allow Fred and his visitors to have the entire pod to themselves. Fred requested me, his father from Florida, and another inmate by the name of James Goff, whom he considered his brother. I was very hesitant to take part in this visitation at first because I decided when I began this research not to meet with any family members. However, I did want to observe what happens to a person in their final days and their actions in response to it. I also wanted to see how the prison staff treated them towards the end.

Before the event, the prison staff told me they would allow Fred, me, and his other visitors to order any food we wanted from local restaurants, and they would have it delivered to us. They told me to bring money and show up to the prison by 8:00 a.m. I showed up as usual, got my ID card and locker outside the reception area, and locked up my keys, wallet, and cell phone. I kept $80 in cash on me since we were going to be ordering out, and I had no idea what to expect. I had never heard of anyone being able to have food delivered to death row before, and it wasn't as though this was Fred's last meal. When I was escorted to where Fred was being held, he sat there and appeared to be very agitated. There were no handcuffs on him, no shackles, and he was free to walk around as much as he wanted, yet he just sat there. I asked him what was wrong, and he told me he was pissed at the warden for not allowing James Goff to be with him during this last visitation. He said the warden hadn't told him about it until just before I got there, and he felt that the warden was doing this to him just to be a prick.

This was the first time I had ever seen Fred so angry. He kept telling me that if the warden came in during the visit, "Don't be surprised if I try and kill that black bastard!"

I was able to calm Fred down by telling him that "it is what it is" and that they were just probably trying to get him to say or do something stupid so they could end his last visitation early. I also reminded him that since his father had just driven up from Florida to see his son for the very last time, he probably didn't really want to ruin that. He agreed with me, and we started talking about how he was holding up. Shortly after we began talking, the guards escorted his father in. When his father walked over to us and sat down, it was the first time I ever felt sorrow on death row. The man in front of me was in his late 70s, and he had just driven nearly twenty hours to see his son for the very last time. They hadn't seen each other for a number of years, but they talked on the phone every week.

I remember thinking, "This man could be my father." The look in his eyes and the sound of his voice echoed defeat. He looked tired, frail, and completely lost. Fred tried to be as upbeat as possible and talked a lot about the old times with his dad, but I could tell that his dad had no idea what to say. He was trying to stay strong, even realizing that he would never see his son alive again. He blamed himself. Once, when Fred went to use the restroom, his father turned to me and said, "His mother and I did the best we could for our kids. I don't understand how or why Fred turned out the way he did."

I told him that some things are never meant to be understood and that people make bad decisions in life. I also told him not to blame himself for his son's actions and not to let this haunt him for the rest of his life. He thanked me for being there with him and told me he wasn't sure if he could have come to death row and sit with Fred all alone.

After a while, Fred called over one of the guards to see about getting the menus for the different restaurants so we could all figure out what we wanted to eat. The guard brought over one menu and said that this place, which was Italian, was the only place we had to choose from. This outraged Fred. His voice became noticeably higher and said that first they took away one of his choices for his last visit, and now they want to take away his food choices. That's when he demanded to see the warden. While waiting for the warden to arrive, Fred's father and I tried to keep Fred as calm as we could so as not to draw any more guards over our way. It was at this time that Fred decided to take off his prison shirt. His entire back was covered with a tattoo of a Klansman in his robe with "KKK" and "White power" written underneath. I'm sure this was a show of power for when the warden, who happened to be black, arrived.

As the warden approached, Fred stood up. A meeting between a black warden and a racist skinhead, days away from being executed, who has repeatedly said he wanted to kill the warden, and who was extremely upset at the moment – I honestly thought that things were going to end badly. As the warden approached, I told Fred to "go easy" and see what he had to say. The warden explained to Fred that the reason for the denial of Goff's visitation with him was because the Department of Corrections policy would not allow another inmate to be a visitor. As for the menu selection, they had some bad experiences in the past with the other places so they decided to stick with this specific place, and they had the best food anyways. After some words were exchanged, Fred seemed to accept the warden's explanation and let it go.

We sat down to look at the menu and then told the guards to call it in. The total amount of the food that we ordered came to nearly $100. The guards told us that they would escort us back to the receiving area so we could go to our lockers on the other side of the prison and get the money to pay for the food when it arrived. Here I was sitting on death row with $80 cash in my pocket that I had no idea I wasn't allowed to have on me. Once again, I realized how easy it would be to smuggle just about anything back to death row since they never really searched us when we came back after the first time. I didn't want the guards to think that I did this on purpose so I just said, "All right." Then I went back with Fred's father and pretended to get the money out of my locker.

When the food arrived, the guards went through it to make sure nothing else was brought in with it; then we ate. The food took up two full tables since Fred ordered just about everything on the menu. We talked about the process for a while, and he asked me questions about what to expect and if I thought it was going to hurt. He explained to me that I was the only person who could really tell him and the others what it's really like the day of an execution since no one comes back. They are basically kept in the dark about the entire process. I explained it to him as best as I could, and that seemed to calm him down some.

Before I knew it, our time was almost up. Those eight hours seem to have flown by for all three of us. I told Fred that I was going to leave first so he could say his last goodbyes to his father. His father was going to be driving back to Florida that night and was having Fred's cremated ashes sent to him after everything was over.

Fred thanked me for everything and gave me a hug. He asked if I would stay in touch with James Goff because James would see to it that I got any information I needed to help out with my research. I told him that I would, and he said, "Well, I guess I'll see you in the death chamber." That was the last time I would speak to Fred. The next time I would see him he would be strapped to the execution table waiting to die.

As I was leaving, I had to remind myself that as nice as Fred was to me, he was still a cold-blooded killer. This man had shot and killed a store clerk, led police officers on a high-speed chase trying to kill them as well, and had robbed and victimized countless people before coming to death row. He even went so far as to tie up women in places that he robbed, take light bulbs, shove them into their vaginas, and kick them before he left. This would cause the light bulbs to shatter inside of the women. Fred Treesh was not someone that you would bring home to dinner.

Fred's execution was the last one that I have witnessed to date. There are other inmates who have asked me to attend their execution; a couple of them are on a stay of execution. One day when I was discussing capital punishment and my work with a good friend and colleague of mine by the name of Paul Sowers, he pointed out that he, like many others, find it fascinating to get a first-hand account of what really goes on during an execution of an inmate. He asked me a question that to this day I still keep asking myself, "So when does your research stop being research and start becoming an obsession?"

I wasn't sure what he meant at first; but when he repeated the question, it really hit me. I had been involved in every aspect of capital punishment now. I had witnessed a man being sentenced to death. I had been to death row countless times and interviewed some of the worst killers in our state's history. I had eaten meals with them and been there when a stay of execution was granted. I have been the last person a condemned man would ever speak to alone, and I have watched men die. From an educational standpoint, there was nothing else that I could learn; yet I kept going back for more. I was doing something in my field of study that no one else has ever really been able to do before. I had devoted years to finding out all I could about death row in the state of Ohio, and realistically I have already accomplished that goal. So why continue? Is it morbid curiosity or an obsession? Deep down I believe I know the answer, but only time will tell if I continue to interview death row inmates and witness their deaths.

CHAPTER 5

THE COUNTDOWN

I will never forget the first execution I ever witnessed. In fact, I will never forget any of the executions I was involved with. I don't know how anyone could forget.

The confidential execution protocol for the state of Ohio details the process in approximately 640 pages (Protocol for the Southern Ohio Correctional Facility, Ohio Department of Rehabilitation and Correction, November 1, 2007). This protocol is never released to the public, but I was fortunate enough to be given a copy by a Common Pleas Court Judge in Ohio. Most of the protocol is very mundane, scientific, and, in my opinion, not very useful in describing what actually goes on during the taking of a human life. Regardless of what method is used during an execution, no two executions are ever alike. Just like there is no such thing as a routine surgery, there is also no such thing as a routine execution.

The actual process begins about thirty days in advance when the condemned inmate is moved from his normal death row cell to a different section still located on death row. He is kept separate from those that were on his pod and placed on suicide watch. I have always found it fascinating how the State of Ohio will go to such great lengths to keep a death row inmate alive long enough to kill them. During this time, the inmate loses many of his privileges and is not free to move about like he was in common quarters. The inmate, however, may choose another inmate to be moved into the separate pod with him in order to have someone to talk to and spend recreation time together.

Also, during the 30-day period prior to the execution, the inmate's scheduled clemency hearing is held. Every inmate that I have dealt with dreads their clemency hearing. Most do not even want to have one, and they certainly do not want to attend it. This is their last and final chance to beg for their life. By this stage of the process, the inmates have typically come to hate humanity so much that the last thing they want to do is beg for mercy. They would rather go out looking tough. Inmates know the chances are almost zero of ever being granted clemency, which would allow them to serve out their sentence in general population. The Clemency Board makes the final recommendation to the Governor to either grant clemency or deny clemency and carry out the sentence of death ("Ohio").

Approximately one week before the scheduled execution, the inmate is moved once again, this time to a much more secluded part of the prison, and he is completely isolated from the rest of the inmates. Here he will stay locked down and all alone with the exception of the guards who now keep an even closer eye on him to ensure that he doesn't do anything to harm himself. Usually during this time, the inmate will write letters, make phone calls to loved ones, and draft his own version of a last will and testament which names those closest to him on death row who will get his personal belongings after the execution is carried out— items such as his television, game systems, typewriter, nude pictures, and anything else acquired over the years on death row. I have found over the years that most, if not all, of the inmates put a great deal of thought into this process. It makes them feel more human. They are very selective about who gets what and for what reason. Of course, no one really knows if the prison officials actually follow through with these requests, but then again, the inmate will never know either ("Ohio").

It is also during this time that the family is notified and asked what their intentions are after the execution. The families may have the body released to them and their own funeral director to have whatever burial procedure they wish or if there is no family around to claim the body or if they refuse to, the state claims the body, in which case the inmate will be buried on prison grounds in the prison cemetery. Most inmates elect to be cremated and their ashes sent home to either a family member or another loved one. Others have private funerals that are kept quiet. Of course, not all go out so quietly. James Filiaggi not only had a complete funeral but also a very large wake, complete with invitations sent out to people all over the state of Ohio. I was told that over 200 people attended. I cannot confirm this myself since I declined to go. I did, however, place the invite in his file.

Approximately thirty-six hours before the scheduled execution, at a time not disclosed to the public, the inmate will be transported from death row to the Southern Correctional Facility in Lucasville. Once there, the inmate is processed and placed inside the death cell. It is here where he will be given his last meal and say his final goodbyes to the people on his list who are allowed to see him the night before his execution ("Ohio").

Lucasville sits on the Ohio and Kentucky border and housed death row from 1972 until 1995. When the riots broke out inside the prison in 1993, the state moved death row out of Lucasville in 1995 (Ohio Death Penalty Information Center) It is a very menacing prison that still houses some of the worst offenders in the state of Ohio. Ironically, sitting directly across the street from the only prison in the State of Ohio that executes people is a high school. Just a block or so down the same road sits Valley Middle School. I would hate sending my son or daughter to a school where every time they looked out of a window they see rows upon rows of razor wire, fences, and walls. While I am sure that this prison boosts this small town's economy and employment, I can't help but wonder what it does to a child growing up and going to a school that sits across from the death chamber.

Family and friends are allowed one last visitation the night before. Typically, they are allowed to remain with the prisoner until around 8:00 p.m. If the inmate desires, a spiritual advisor may stay with them longer. It is also during this last evening that the condemned inmate will be allowed to eat his last meal which he has ordered prior to being transported down to the death house. One inmate that I have interviewed over the years by the name of Rick Bays has requested that I be there with him during his last meal. In fact, he told me that he doesn't think he will be too hungry so he said I could order whatever I wanted to eat for his last meal. He would rather just talk to me while I ate. As of this time, the execution date has not been set; but I am not sure if the prison would even allow this ("Ohio").

Some states, such as in Texas, will serve whatever is on the regular prison menu for the day for the inmate's last meal (Memmott). Ohio still allows the inmate to order whatever they desire, within reason ("Ohio"). All of my inmate's last meals were pretty much normal meals like steak or chicken, with the exception of Chris Newton's. He wanted two large T-bone steaks with all of the extras and as close to raw as possible. He wanted to be able to see and taste the blood coming out of the meat as he ate. Some just wanted desserts like ice cream or cake. Frank Spisak wanted spaghetti; and when I spoke to him just before his execution, he told me how he only requested a little spaghetti and a piece of chocolate cake, but the guards were so generous that they gave him an entire cake and a pound of spaghetti with all of the extras. He was very grateful for how well he was treated in the death cell.

In fact, every one of the inmates that I have interviewed just prior to their executions have always complimented the warden and staff at Lucasville for how well they were treated during the last full day of their lives. Perhaps it is due to the professionalism of the staff or maybe it is due to the fact that the staff are people who know they are participating in taking a human being's life, and they feel emotional. Most of the guards have said to me that it is just another day to them, but I suspect that when everything is all said and done it is more than just another day to them. At least I hope so. If it is really just another day to them, what does that say about our society? Have we really gotten to the point where taking another person's life, no matter what they have done has become so routine that it is just like any other day? God, I hope not.

CHAPTER 6

"KILLER ART"

The following pictures are of actual artwork that has been given to me by various inmates on Ohio's Death Row. Some are oil paintings on canvas. Some are drawings done in ink or pencil. One is painted using oil-based paints on a white handkerchief. The wood clock was also made on death row. It does work and runs on batteries. The shrunken head is made from dried fruit and material from sweatpants.

All of these pieces of art were hand crafted and shipped to me from death row. All of the materials that were needed to complete these art projects are available to every inmate on Ohio's Death Row. The inmates are allowed to purchase any and all art supplies they wish. Most inmates try to sell their art to willing buyers on the outside, and people will often pay hundreds of dollars per painting. People will also buy signed letters, cards, and just about anything else that the inmates are willing to sell. If an inmate is not allowed to receive money, they will have other inmates broker their artwork for a small fee put in their account. Others will enlist people on the outside to sell the artwork for them and have those individuals deposit the money in their accounts or just purchase the goods they want for them. I have been asked to sell artwork for some inmates for a 60/40 split with 60% to me and 40% to them. I have never sold any artwork for any inmate on death row.

Chris Newton's gift to me just prior to his execution.

David Allen's painting on canvas using his own semen to paint with.

David Allen's canvas painting of a nature scene.

Art work from Ohio's death row (Jose Loza)

Art work from Ohio's death row (Jose Loza)

CHAPTER 7

DATE WITH DEATH

Executions in the state of Ohio take place at 10:00 a.m ("Ohio"). Executions used to take place on a Thursday morning to allow those on the execution team to have a longer weekend off. For whatever reason, that changed, and now they take place on Tuesday mornings ("Ohio"). Since my home is about a four-hour drive to the prison, I usually get there the night before and stay at a local hotel. I am grateful for the lengthy drive because it allows me the solitude needed to process what is about to take place and then to clear my head after the execution is over. The day before I leave to go to an execution, I usually keep my son home from school. I don't explain to him why, and I certainly do not call the school and tell them the reason for his absence is a scheduled execution. I usually just let him sleep in and when he wakes up, I tell him I got him out of school, and we just go out. Sometimes we go shopping or out to eat. I don't plan the day, but it is something I do to take my mind off of things. I am so thankful to be able to spend time with him like this knowing that so many others do not get this opportunity. It also helps to ease his worries about me because my family is always on edge each time that I go to death row and especially to an execution.

I arrive at the prison at 6:30 a.m. I am met by a guard who has most of the parking blocked off. The Ohio State

Highway Patrol surrounds the front of the prison complex. They are in charge of everything that occurs outside of the prison walls. The parking lot is usually divided in half, one side for those protesting in favor of the death penalty and one side for those protesting against the death penalty. That end of the prison parking lot is where the gates open up to allow the hearse to drive in and out that will eventually contain the body of the executed inmate. The number of protesters that show up generally depends on the weather. If it is nice outside, more people show up to demonstrate than when the weather is lousy.

I park in the section reserved for the witnesses so we are shielded from the protesters and the media, who generally have cameras set up. When I enter the prison, I walk through a metal detector and sign in. I am given a badge that identifies me as a witness to the execution, and I wait for an escort to the briefing room. The room has a conference table and chairs and looks and feels very prison-like. Attorneys for the defendant gather here as well as any clergy the defendant may have requested. The windows in this room look directly at the death house.

Witnesses for the prosecution, the prosecutor of the original case and the victim's family wait in a separate briefing room. Typically, the witnesses for the state are victims or family. No more than three witnesses are allowed for the state and for the defendant. I cannot say what goes on in their briefing room since I have always been kept in the room holding the defense attorneys and clergy. The witnesses for the state never see me although, when it is time to be escorted to the death chamber, they are led over first, and I can see through the window exactly who the three witnesses are.

One might think that the atmosphere in the briefing room is solemn and tense, as witnesses wait for a last-minute stay of execution. However, inmates are considered a volunteer if they forgo any of their last appeals. Every experience I have had has been the same. Attorneys discuss where they stayed the night before and who had what for dinner. The clergy talk about their parishes and, somewhere in between, why capital punishment doesn't work. I sit back and take note of everything being said. I only speak when spoken to, and even then, I keep my responses to a bare minimum.

Usually no one asks me who I am for the first hour or so. I think they assume that I am prison staff since there are usually two staff members in the room to explain the protocol for the day. When someone does ask me what my role is, I explain that I am there to witness the death of the defendant and write about it later. Everyone gets quiet then. I can feel their nervousness. The look on their faces when they learn that I have been taking notes on their conversations is priceless. Now they reflect on what they have said out loud and wonder what I am going to say about them. I let them work things out and just sit and write. The second time I attended an execution, the defense attorney got a little heated when I refused to say what I was writing. At one point he looked at me and said, "You sure do write down a lot of stuff," to which I politely replied, "You sure do talk a lot." He didn't speak to me after that.

While in the briefing room, the prison staff tells us when we will be taken over to the death house and when, if everything goes accordingly, we will return to the briefing room. During this time, the media ask the staff to ask whether any of us would be willing to talk to the press afterwards. I have refused all interviews following an execution.

During this time, the defendant is being held inside the death cell which is located inside the death house. The death house is a small brick building that sits completely free from the rest of the prison. It is close to the fences but still inside the prison yard. The condemned inmate can have his spiritual advisor with him during this time if he desires, or he can request to see his attorney or myself. Frank Spisak requested that I be the last person that he would speak to before being put to death. When it was time for me to see Frank, it was 7:50 a.m. I was escorted to the death house by one prison staff member. It is not a far walk from the briefing room; but the moment I step into the prison yard, it feels like an eternity to get there. The entire prison is on lockdown the day of an execution, and the other inmates get restless. Cells surround the yard, and all the inmates with windows facing it yell and scream at you when you step out into the yard. I can never make out what any of them are saying, but it puts me in the mind of the Roman Coliseum and crowds yelling to those entering. It almost feels like I am on display and every single prisoner hates me for being there to watch one of their own executed.

With Spisak, I was given from 7:50 a.m. until 8:20 a.m. The death cell is an extremely small and completely open cell with a bed, toilet, and small writing desk. Three guards sit directly behind me, and one guard sits off to my left typing every single thing that is said between us. Frank thanked me for everything and said he really hoped he helped me out during our time together on death row. He hoped it would keep others from ever coming to death row. Then he said something that I thought was very strange for a man about to die. He told me I really looked more like a lawyer, dressed better and was more professional than any of his attorneys. I thanked him and wished him well and wondered how a man, who, in less than two hours, would be strapped to an execution table with lethal drugs running through his veins, could be so complementary towards me and wish me all the best. It appeared as though the only care in the world he had was, not for his certain death or his victims, but to make sure I had a good drive back home.

When I was escorted back to the briefing room, his attorneys asked me all kinds of questions. They also asked me to turn over the pictures Frank gave me along with the final judgment that was faxed to him while I was with him that denied his last appeal. His attorneys did not like it when

I told them that since they were Frank's property and that he personally gave them to me for my own use, they were not entitled to any of them. They disliked me even more when I told them they could file a motion with the court or have the documents subpoenaed, but by the time that was processed, their client would be long gone. Needless to say, I still have those documents in my possession.

Sometimes I wonder if any state appointed death row attorney knows anything at all about the law or the protocol for capital punishment. I will never forget the one female attorney for Fred Treesh. It was 9:10 a.m. the morning of his execution. Everyone had seen Fred for the very last time; and in approximately forty-five minutes, the first of the witnesses were to be led over. This is when she looked at me and the other staff and asked, "Do they ever start these early, or do they wait until 10:00 a.m. on the dot?"

I was floored. It seems as though a death row attorney should be fighting for her client's life, yet instead she acted like she had more important places to be. Shouldn't she know what takes place during an execution? More importantly, shouldn't she be trying to push the time back instead of hoping the state kills her client sooner?

The protocol for the beginning of each execution seems to be consistent. At 9:55 a.m., the witnesses for the state are led from the briefing room, across the yard, into the death house. At 10:00 a.m., it's time for me, a spiritual advisor, and one attorney for the defendant to be led over. Inside the death chamber, the room is divided by a half-wall with three small chairs on each side. In front of us less than two feet away is a large plate glass window covered by a curtain. Standing behind us are various members of the media busy writing. They are never allowed to speak to any of us inside of the death chamber. From the moment that you sit down until the moment you leave, the only sounds you hear are pencils moving on paper or your heart beating in your throat. The silence inside of the death chamber is almost deafening.

This is where the consistency stops.

No two executions are ever the same. The end result for them all is ultimately death; however, the process of achieving that end has been different each time in front of me.

Once witnesses are seated, a live, closed-circuit video appears on a television screen mounted in the top left corner of the room. Here, witnesses watch the defendant lay on a table in the next room. From an overhead view, one can see needles inserted into their veins. The audience watches as nervous EMTs try to find a vein on their first try, but it never happens. Once the needles are in place and secured, the television monitor goes off, the curtain opens up, and the condemned inmate is forced to walk the sixteen or so steps from that room to the actual execution chamber. After a step up, they lie down on the execution table and are strapped down by the execution team with straps around ankles, wrists, legs, and chest. Once the inmate is secured, two of the guards on the execution team connect the IV lines that are fed through a small hole in the wall to the IV ports on the inmate's arms. Those lines transport the lethal drugs into the inmate in order to kill him. The executioner is always concealed behind the wall and is never to be seen by us or the public. The executioner who delivers the drugs to kill the inmate is not a trained professional, not a doctor or an anesthesiologist. They are simply a member of the prison staff execution team.

According to the Ohio state training manual, the execution team meets weekly in the month prior to a scheduled execution and rehearses what will happen during the real execution. There is nothing in the written training manual about qualifications for the staff on the execution team. In fact, when an opening comes up, according to the state's own protocol, the announcement is made at roll call to the guards on three consecutive days, and it is also posted by their time clock. Anyone interested in becoming a part of the execution team simply applies. At my first execution, I was able to ask one of the team members why anyone would want to be on the team that kills another human being. His response shocked me. He stated that most do it because they get an extra day off with pay. The trading of a human life for eight hours of pay doesn't really seem worth it to me.

The drugs used in today's lethal injections vary from state to state and also from death to death. There has been so much controversy about which drugs to use and how to obtain them that some states are considering going back to the methods used before lethal injection became an option. In Ohio, the main method of execution used to be electrocution. In fact, up until a few years ago, the inmate had to fill out a form called "Election of Manner of Execution" and choose either death by lethal injection or death by electrocution. If the inmate did not file this form one week ahead of their scheduled execution, then they would automatically be executed in the electric chair.

As of 2015, the state of Ohio still has a ban on executions until a new drug protocol can be adopted and accepted by the courts. It is not because states cannot figure out which drugs to use, but rather that the drug companies, once they find out that their drugs are being used for executions, stop production or stop supplying them to the Department of Corrections.

For the longest time until January 2014 (Associated Press, Julie Carr Smyth, 10/10/15), Ohio used a three-drug cocktail protocol for lethal injection. A combination of thiopental sodium, pancuronium bromide, and potassium chloride were delivered in succession to kill the inmate.

Once the inmate is led into the death chamber and strapped to the table, the warden asks them if they have any last statement to give before they are put to death. My very first execution was probably my worst. Not only did it take close to two hours from start to finish to execute the inmate, but I had no idea what to expect and when anything would happen. No one announced when the procedure is started. As you sit mere feet away from someone strapped down in front of you, watching them watch you or the phone on the wall, wondering if it will ring to stop the execution, you never quite know when the drugs are being administered. I later found out in the state's protocol that the warden lets the executioner know to start the execution simply by buttoning his top button on his suit coat. This remains the same signal today. When the warden buttons his coat, it is time to die.

When the executioner gets the signal, the first drug is administered. Two grams of thiopental sodium with 25 mg/cc concentration for a total of 80 cc are delivered from two syringes. As the drugs flow, the inmate usually falls asleep rather quickly. After the first drug is administered, a saline flush is pushed through the IV lines to clear the way for the second drug to be delivered. The saline flush takes approximately one minute. The second drug, 100 mg of pancuronium bromide with 2 mg/ml concentration for a total of 50 cc is delivered from two syringes. This drug is intended to paralyze the inmate so that his natural defense mechanisms will not be noticeable to the witnesses. It appears that he is lying there peacefully when in fact he just cannot move. This is a fast-acting drug; however, if a person is large, as in the case of Chris Newton, the drug does not last long. This is why I not only heard Newton gasping for air: I saw his entire chest and abdominal area convulse. Another flush of saline is used to clear the lines before the final drug, 100 milliequivalents of potassium chloride with 2 mg/cc concentration for a total of 50 cc, is pushed through the IV lines. This drug causes the heart to go into a cardiac arrest. The heart stops giving the inmate a fatal heart attack. If all goes as planned, the inmate is usually dead within fifteen to twenty minutes from the administration of the first drug.

I have no idea if the inmate is mentally aware of what's going on during this process so I can't tell you for certain if it is a painless death or not. The United States Constitution protects us from cruel and unusual punishment. Nowhere does it say that an execution should not hurt.

Once the warden checks the inmate for a pulse and shakes him a couple of times, the curtain closes. A medical doctor enters the death chamber to verify that there are no vital signs and to pronounce him dead. The doctor then leaves the chamber, and the curtain is opened to mark the time of death in front of the witnesses. The defendants' three witnesses are led out first, followed by the states' three witnesses. We are all escorted back to our assigned briefing rooms while the media is taken to their separate assigned room. All witnesses on both sides, as well as anyone else that was permitted to be in the briefing rooms but not allowed to witness the execution, are held there until the body is loaded into the hearse. The reason for this is to allow those family members who were not chosen to witness the execution to be able to see that the execution has in fact taken place and the inmate is no longer alive. The hearse is then driven out across the yard, through the gates, and past everyone who has gathered outside of the prison to demonstrate.

The hearse that was waiting on Chris Newton's body was so old it did not look like it would run. In fact, when I mentioned it to one of the prison staff members as we were heading over to the death-house, he told me that one time it didn't start and had to be jumped. There was talk among the inmates housed at the prison that they were going to take up a collection in order to get a battery for that hearse. I'm not sure if that ever occurred, but I do know that I never saw that hearse again.

CHAPTER 8

A SYSTEM BROKEN

Day after day I am constantly asked, "Are you for or against the death penalty?" People get upset with me because I never give them a straight answer. The fact of the matter is that my belief on this issue is completely irrelevant. I never set out to try and convince people one way or the other, and it was certainly never my goal to change people's minds about the death penalty.

My ultimate goal has been to bring forth the most accurate information that I can as a firsthand witness. I want people to see the information I have obtained and use their own critical thinking skills to make an educated decision to support or not support capital punishment in the state of Ohio and around the country.

To say that our system of capital punishment is broken or flawed is an understatement. I don't disagree with people who say that the death penalty should be used. However, I can't agree when those same people argue that the death penalty is a deterrent. Over the years I have come face to face with some of the lowest forms of the human species. Some are so evil and dangerous there really is no place for them to live in society. The more pertinent question is, how do we remove them from our society? I have come to realize that it is the most difficult question to answer. No one, from the justices on the United States Supreme Court to the elected county prosecutors, can ever seem to agree, which is most likely the major breakdown in our system. The capital punishment issue does not escape our also flawed political system. It is sad that in our civilized society today that we still have people running for elected office that use capital punishment as one of their platforms to get elected. The very thought of people trying to win the votes of others simply by pushing for the right to take the lives of others in the name of justice, in my professional opinion, is almost criminal in and of itself.

I am neither completely against the death penalty or completely opposed to it. I'm only hoping to understand why and educate others about the failure of the system. There is almost nothing organized or professional in the way we hand down a sentence of death to someone. I'm not speaking only of the method by which they are actually executed, I am also speaking of the judicial system as a whole.

One of the inmates whose execution I witnessed was on our death row for twenty-eight years. Another one was only on death row for five years. How can this be?

In the state of Ohio, if a defendant is being tried for a capital murder case and has no money for a lawyer, the court must appoint two attorneys to represent them. Those attorneys must be death penalty certified. This means that those attorneys have gone through specific training after law school and have sat on previous death penalty cases. They are usually very knowledgeable about the law and have practiced for a number of years.

However, there are no qualifications or experience requirements for a judge in a murder trial. The one person who can actually sentence an individual to death can be someone with no experience whatsoever in capital punishment. In fact, it's possible that a newly elected judge could have a capital murder case as their very first trial. Judges can be appointed to the bench through political party favors, or they can be voted in by popularity or by outspending their competition. Yet they are the ones to hand down a sentence of death to another human being. How is this right? How is this justified?

In the state of Ohio, there are eighty-eight counties. Each county has an elected County Prosecutor. He or she holds the ultimate power as to whether a person should face the death penalty. Only they can decide to seek the death penalty or ask for a life sentence without parole. Of the eighty-eight counties, thirty-two counties have sentenced people to die as of today. Twelve of these counties have only one person on death row compared to the likes of Hamilton County, which houses twenty-five inmates on death row, and Cuyahoga County, which has twenty-three inmates waiting to die.

I'm not sure how many of the elected prosecutors throughout the state have ever been to death row or has witnessed an actual execution, but my guess is not too many. Maybe if more prosecutors did visit our states' death row and see firsthand how well they are treated there, then I would be willing to bet that when the family members of a slain victim inquires about the death penalty, the county prosecutor's response would be totally different. How in good conscience can any elected official sit down with family members who have just lost a loved one or even many loved ones, look them straight in the eye, and tell them that seeking the death penalty would be in their best interest? How does he or she explain to them that based on the laws in Ohio, criminals sentenced to death will have to wait approximately eighteen to twenty years to see their sentence carried out. During that time, the condemned killer will be allowed unlimited visits from their family and friends, have hand-held video games, a television, around-the-clock medical care including mental health treatment, art supplies, food boxes, and the freedom to move around to socialize with others.

In the meantime, the victim's family will have to follow the defendant's appeal process in order to know what is going on. They will have to constantly relive their experiences each time an appeal is filed. They will never reach the last closure point until after the killer is eventually executed, if they ever are. The anticipation, waiting, and stress these families endure seems to me like cruel and unusual punishment that is being inflicted on them by the state. This was told directly to me by some of the victims' families that I have come into contact with over the years.

For one of my scheduled executions, I made arrangements for someone to cover my classes, kept my son home from school the day before like always, made my hotel reservations, and was ready to leave when I received notice that the governor granted a thirty day stay of execution. I remember how unsettled I felt when I got the news, which I only received because I called the prison one last time to confirm everything, and they told me that a stay had been ordered. I didn't know whether to be upset because of the wasted effort to prepare for the trip or happy because I didn't have to see another human being die the next day.

I learned that some of the victim's family members came from California to witness the execution of Kenneth Smith. They had waited two decades and flown over 2,000 miles to Ohio at their own expense, only to be told that a stay was granted. To make matters worse, since the state of Ohio schedules executions so far in advance, once a stay is granted, that person goes back to the bottom of the list, pushing back the execution as much as a couple of years. I cannot figure out how justice is being served when a condemned inmate and the state of Ohio have such control over the lives of the victims.

It is my personal and professional opinion that this system is broken in so many ways that in order to fix it, the entire process from beginning to end needs to be completely overhauled. More emphasis needs to be placed on victims and their families and not on prosecutors. Death row needs to be more transparent, and executions need to be less secretive. The public deserves to know exactly what takes place before, during, and after an execution. Currently, the state is protecting the rights of condemned inmates at the emotional and material expense of victims, their families, and the general public.

The days of public executions are, thankfully, long gone. However, I have often speculated whether there would be an audience in today's society for public executions. If people are willing to pay $50 to watch wrestling, cage fighting, or boxing on television, then how implausible is it that morbid curiosity would motivate people to watch an execution? While the profits from a pay-per-view execution could bring financial relief to victims and their families, I cannot advocate for this type of brutal and barbaric public display.

However, the general public deserves to know the truth about the correctional system and the execution process.

It is going to take a lot more than a book like this to change the process of handing down the ultimate sentence of death. If people start questioning elected officials, then perhaps the necessary changes could be made. Politicians are resistant to change unless change is forced upon them. The public needs to force that change by calling, emailing, or writing letters to their prosecutors, judges, state representatives, and governor. Here are some suggestions of questions that interested voters might ask elected officials:

•—Are you educated on the death penalty? How did you become knowledgeable about it?

•—Have you ever visited death row or witnessed an execution personally?

•—Do you keep in contact with victim's families in the same way you keep an eye on inmate appeals?

•—What is your personal belief about the death penalty?

•—Do you think a death sentence is worth all the years of grief and despair that the victims' families will have to face?

•—Can you justify the special treatment given to inmates on death row compared to the grief and torment of the victim's family?

The ultimate question is, is it really worth it? I cannot answer for victims or family members of victims because I have never had to face such tragedy. However, after devoting the last seven and a half years of my life to learning every possible detail that I could about death row, the inmates, and the execution process, I can honestly say that the way the system works right now, no. It is not worth it.

CHAPTER 9

WHERE ARE THEY NOW

Since I first started this dark and twisted journey inside the cell blocks of Ohio's death row in 2007, a lot has changed. Death row was once again on the path to being moved from Chillicothe to the maximum-security prison located in the City of Toledo. The inmates on death row were completely against this move as it would have infringed on their "lifestyle" that they had all along in Chillicothe. They would no longer be able to have as much recreational time, fewer showers, and most certainly less freedoms that they have grown so accustomed to when they were first transferred to the oldest prison in the state. I remember the inmates telling me during interviews that they were going to fight this move all the way to the top. The prison had gone so far as to determine how the inmates were to be transferred, how many would be transferred on each trip, and even held up their packages being delivered so that they would not get lost in the move. My guys would explain to me that they were not told when they would be moved but only that the guards were going to eventually come in around 3:00 in the morning and tell them to roll out. This would be the sign that they were going to be moved to their new home. The reason they would never disclose the date to them, or anyone else for that matter, was due to the security threat. Moving over 140 of the state's worst known killers on different buses for a 4-hour ride over state highways, one could easily see how many things could go wrong. Can you imagine if even one bus full of condemned killers were to have broken down, had an accident, or even hijacked? Not only would the entire state of Ohio and the surrounding states be at risk, imagine how the families of the victims would feel knowing that their loved one's killer was free to seek whatever revenge they could on them! Now many people might think that this would be an exaggerated scenario; however, one death row inmate in particular wanted to do just that. This brings me to William Sapp.

William Sapp, who was discussed in the first edition, is still currently on Ohio's death row awaiting his execution, which he has asked me to attend. He still fantasizes about getting out one day. On July 4th of 2017, myself and a film production company from London, England, were in Springfield, Ohio, filming for what was supposed to be a series about him and others on death row that I have interviewed over the years. We were in Springfield after wrapping up two full days of filming at our home in Sandusky. It was miserably hot outside. It was 90+ degrees out, humid, and of course no air conditioning on due because it was interfering with the sound. We were talking to residents about the senseless murders of two young girls that were committed by Sapp. The girls, who were only twelve years old at the time, were abducted right off of the street, taken in to a wooded area that also contained a spring filled pond, and savagely murdered. Their heads were bashed in to the point of being unrecognizable. They were then discarded with some branches and other debris tossed on top of them. Sapp would tell me one time during an interview with him on death row that he decided to kill them because they were in "his area" and that he did not like it when others came around to his spots.

So, after a long day of filming and feeling this sense of worthlessness for having to dredge up old memories in a small town about such brutal crimes, we go back to the hotel room to set up for a live interview with Sapp via video. It was during this interview that I asked him if he ever thought about what it would be like to be free and if he thought he would just go off into the woods in Alaska or somewhere and forget all about society after being where he has for the last thirteen years. He was very matter of fact when he spoke and stated without hesitation that, "If I were to ever get out, if the walls came down in a tornado or something like that which would give me the opportunity to escape, I would go straight back to my hometown of Springfield and finish what I started!" When I asked him what he meant by that, he said, "To go back and finish killing the family members of those I killed so I could wipe out the bloodline." I remember looking back at the director and camera operator, and they had this look on their faces as if they just saw the Devil in real life. Little did they know that they did in fact see the Devil in human form.

The filming wrapped up after five grueling days which were made into a 10-minute sizzle reel to shop to the different networks. As luck would have it, the way networks work at their own pace and, of course, COVID entering the scene, nothing ever materialized. I have continued to interview William Sapp to this day, and he has provided me with locations to three separate bodies of victims that he killed and has not been charged for. He also states and has maintained ever since I have known him to be the killer of another victim in which a different guy is on Ohio's death row for the murder of, yet no one will listen to him. I will continue to gain whatever information I can from him for as long as I can so that hopefully one day, there might just be some closure for other families out there. Meanwhile, "Wild Bill," as he is called, still sits on Ohio's death row patiently waiting for his "state sanctioned murder" as he puts it and continues to do various arts and crafts as shown in the pictures that follow. He has also asked that I attend his execution when it is scheduled (as you can see here in his letter to me); and as it stands, I will probably be there to watch him die as well.

William Sapp's description of the location to (1) of his victims yet to be discovered. (see full resolution letters and forms at **wbp.bz/wmdgallery***)*

*On location with the film crew at a location
to one of Sapp's undiscovered victims.*

*Film Crew on location at Kimberlin's
working on Sapp's location of victims.*

Another one of the inmates that I was first to interview on Ohio's death row was Anthony Sowell, AKA "The Cleveland Strangler." Toney, as he liked to be called, was placed on death row for the brutal and senseless murders and dismemberment of eleven completely innocent women from the Cleveland area. Sowell not only preyed upon and killed these women, he also cut many of them up, buried them in his back yard, and even had the remains of some inside of his home at the time of his arrest. He was the stereotypical serial killer when it came to his actions and his words. He was arrogant, thought he was smarter than everyone else, and craved the attention. In fact, the reason why he and I ended our communications was due to the fact that he wanted me to focus solely on him and no one else on death row during my research. He told me numerous times that he wanted to be known as the "most notorious serial killer on death row." Whenever I would mention to him that I was interviewing others on death row, he would get upset. He really got upset one day when I was on death row, and I was scheduled to interview him from 8:00 a.m.-12:00 p.m., and then I was scheduled to interview another inmate from 1:00 p.m.-5:00 p.m. He could not understand why I could not just stay and speak to him for the eight hours. He stated that if I were going to continue to talk to other guys on death row then I could just forget about his story all together. He also wanted me to pay him for his story as well, in which I also respectfully declined.

Sowell would go on to tell me how close he was to the Mayor of Cleveland (Frank Jackson) before all the murders took place and that he not only dated the mayor's niece but had been to his house several times. He would also talk about how he was "gifted" in many areas as a child but never felt like he could win the affection of his mother that he so desperately longed for. He gave me countless pages of paperwork showing his service in the United States Marine Corps and boasted about being a "world traveler." Of course, in true form, anytime I would bring up his previous rape conviction where he did his time in the same institution he was now sitting in, he would deflect that conversation. Just as he would when I would ask him if there were more victims not known to law enforcement. While he would admit to having a daughter, he would not discuss his ex-wife who he claimed died many years ago in an industrial accident, of which I could never confirm. He would also not say where his daughter was, her age, and the last time they had communication. Eventually, our conversations ceased as he began to get more and more upset at the fact that I would not give him all of the attention. In my mind, I saw him more as an adolescent behaving like a child instead of a serial killer acting like a monster. He would tell me in one of his letters that the painting he had done specifically for me of eleven tombstones with the names of the victims on each one, he was selling to someone so that I wouldn't have it. Instead, I have these "bloody handprints" on canvas with his thumbprint and signature on the back (pictured, next page). Although the communication between the two of us would end, I was always told by other inmates that he would often ask about me and see what all I was writing about. In fact, I was told by one of the guys on death row that he had done three other paintings that were in his cell and set aside for me. Those paintings were never to arrive. In March 2021, Anthony Sowell died of cancer while still awaiting his execution on death row. Several other death row inmates and I had known that he was diagnosed with cancer well over a year ago and that he was not going to accept any treatment for it. And while I was left to wonder if there were other victims out there who will forever go undiscovered, I was also left with a sense of relief that this once physically intimidating former Marine was left to waste away and suffer a longer and more agonizing death than the needle could have ever done. It was only fitting.

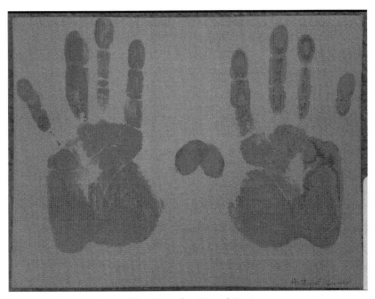

Anthony Sowell's Bloody Hand-Prints on canvas.

Ohio's death penalty under the current administration of Governor Mike DeWine has ceased to exist. Those who are in favor of abolishing the capital punishment, on the surface, may see this as a victory or at least a step in the right direction to ending it all together. Those in favor of the death penalty see this as little more than a political cop-out. A Republican Governor that is too afraid to lose the support of his base if he decides to abolish it altogether instead blames it on the inability to procure the correct lethal drugs in order to carry out the method of execution so that it doesn't amount to cruel and unusual punishment. Who is right and who is wrong here? I would say both. On the one hand, for those who want to abolish the death penalty in the state of Ohio, any moratorium that stops the executions from going forward is a step in the right direction. Governor DeWine has stated that he will not move forward with the death penalty while he is in office and while the only method is lethal injection due to the fact that "Ohio cannot secure the needed lethal injection drugs to carry out the executions properly." He also stated that lawmakers in Ohio "must choose a different method of execution (such as lethal gas or firing squad) to resume capital punishment" (Randy Ludlow, The Columbus Dispatch, 12/16/2020). The state of Ohio last executed an inmate in July 2018. Governor DeWine has not allowed an execution to go forward since he took office.

It is well known that those who align themselves with the Republican Party tend to favor capital punishment while those who align themselves with the Democratic Party tend to favor doing away with the death penalty all together. Of course, this is not true for everyone, but generally speaking. This is what makes this debate so politically polarizing between the two parties. We just saw the state of Virginia abolish the death penalty completely in 2021. A state that was known for its heavy use of the death penalty in the past and until recently was also known to be a Republican state. This is what makes Ohio seem like the odd state out. Prior to Governor DeWine taking office in 2019, we had Governor John Kasich, who was a Republican, and prior to Governor Kasich, we had Governor Ted Strickland, who was not only a Democrat but also worked in the prison system. He and Governor Kasich both oversaw executions carried out in the state using the same exact lethal injection process; yet when Governor DeWine took office, he was quick to conclude that the process used in Ohio was not going to be used on his watch. It was during his term that while he stated that the process was no longer going to be utilized due to not being able to secure the drugs needed to carry the executions out, the Federal Government under the administration of President Trump, was set to carry out the most executions of any sitting President in modern times. This also included the execution of the only female death row inmate housed on Federal death row (Lisa Montgomery), who happened to be one that I had interviewed for several years and was supposed to attend the execution of as well but, due to COVID-19, was not permitted. She was the first female executed by the

United States Federal Government in nearly seventy years. In total, President Trump's administration carried out thirteen Federal Executions in Terre Haute, Indiana, all by lethal injection, with the last one completed on January 16, 2021 (Jonathan Allen, Bhargav Acharya, Reuters, 01/16/2021). It had been seventeen years since the last Federal inmate was put to death, and President George Bush Sr. was in the Oval Office at the time. We now had thirteen people put to death in the state of Indiana, by the Federal Government, in a state that borders Ohio, by the same method of execution as Ohio yet the drugs were not able to be "secured" for Ohio to move forward. One must question the validity of the Governor's decision to end the executions solely on this basis alone.

Governor DeWine has not, however, ended the death penalty for good. This is where those who are in favor of capital punishment may also claim victory. All it would take is electing another governor to the statehouse who also favors capital punishment and the de-facto moratorium could easily be lifted. In fact, changing the method of the execution from lethal injection to either firing squad or lethal gas as the current governor had suggested would be much more difficult than just re-instating the ultimate form of punishment of death by a newly elected governor. All he or she would have to do is lift the stay and set the dates. At that point, all of the nearly 140 men and one woman on Ohio's death row would be looking at a date with death. Of those, I have been asked by at least six to witness their executions if and when they are given their execution date. Cleveland Jackson, David Allen, and Charles Lorraine are three such inmates housed in Chillicothe that I have interviewed since "Watch Me Die" was first released. Their stories, like all of them on death row, end in tragic death.

The Other Inmates:

Cleveland Jackson, a short but personable guy on death row, has seen his date of execution come and go more than once. He was scheduled to die on November 13, 2019, and I was set to meet with him one last time at the death house before witnessing his execution until Governor DeWine gave him a reprieve. Jackson was granted this stay by the Governor due to "Mr. Jackson's poor legal representation and evidence of Mr. Jackson's intellectual disability that was not developed and presented at the appropriate time" (Cleveland Plain Dealer, September 30, 2019). His execution was rescheduled for January 13, 2021. He remains alive and still on death row today.

I cannot speak as to whether Jackson was fairly represented at trial since I am not an attorney, and I cannot say if he suffers from any intellectual disabilities either. What I can say is that based on my interactions with him over the years, he appeared to be very well spoken, well groomed, very polite, and understood exactly what he did and why.

When I first met Cleveland, he shocked me by how short and happy he was. He liked to smile. He also liked to talk, a lot. We would sit and eat and discuss everything from the conditions of prison to how others acted on death row. I distinctly remember him talking about one guy on his pod (whom I refuse to say his name), who happens to be from my hometown and is awaiting his execution for the murders of a beautiful young woman and two little babies.

This particular inmate had already served nearly thirteen years for killing another young woman prior to killing these three. Cleveland Jackson would tell me how other guys on the pod would get so mad at this guy for "always being drunk and smoking weed." Not that getting drunk or high offended Jackson, or anyone else on death row for that matter, but because he would get too loud and obnoxious. To the point where the guards would eventually have to do something about it, which usually meant that they would crack down on everyone. That is why the others did not like him.

We talked about how his life was thrown away by "living the fast life" of selling drugs, robbing people, and doing whatever was necessary to get by. It was this very lifestyle that landed him where he was and talking to me. He was sentenced to death on August 5, 2002, for the murders of a three-year-old and a seventeen-year-old when he and his step-brother decided to shoot everyone during a botched drug deal. There were six people inside the apartment that Cleveland Jackson and his stepbrother went over to. All six people were shot, all but one were minors, two died from their gunshot wounds. I asked Jackson about the deaths of those he shot and how he felt about it. He, like most on death row do, minimized his actions and behaviors. He didn't say he was innocent, but he did try to make excuses as to why things went down the way they did. He explained to me over lunch that the baby should have never been shot. I asked him what he meant by that and he told me that it was the "other victim's fault." Now when people ask me, and they do all the time, "what is the hardest part of interviewing killers," most people expect me to say "when they tell me about the gory details of their crimes" or "when they tell me in graphic detail about sexually assaulting the victim before and after they kill them," but the truth is, when they start to blame their senseless acts on someone else or even hint that it was the victim's fault, that is when I have to put on my game face and pretend not to get upset. This is when I must convince myself not to just get up and leave. So I stay and listen. Jackson went on to explain that while he and his brother did go over there to rob them of their money, he did not know it was going to end up in murder. He could not really say why it happened other than things "just went south." I pressed him on the issue of the little three-year-old and how that all happened and that is when he went on to explain that he did mean to shoot the other person; but when he started shooting, the seventeen-year-old held up the baby like it was a shield or something. The next thing he knew "the baby took one to the head." He then went on to say, in an agitated voice, "I didn't want to shoot that kid, but who holds a kid up for protection anyway?" "If they wouldn't have held that little kid up, they'd still be alive today." Both the three-year-old and the seventeen-year-old were killed.

Cleveland, like most of the inmates I talk to on death row is always concerned for my health, my family, and making sure that I am all right and if I need anything. When I was first introduced to this behavior from guys on death row, I was fascinated by the fact that here are all these brutal killers, who could care a less about the ones they murdered or their families, yet they are so concerned about me and mine. I have since come to the realization that in doing so, this is what makes them feel "more like a human being and less like a monster." In their mind, they finally have someone who is not judging them, is not always giving them an opinion, and is willing to learn from them. It is less about me, more about them. They like the idea that they are allowed to act like a caregiver and want to be seen as such. Of course, their true self will always come out in one way or another. It can be in letter form, in the form of art, or even out of their own mouths when they speak. Cleveland was no good at art (his words, not mine), but he could talk and write. Behind that bright smile lies a cold-hearted killer. Able to differentiate between right and wrong. Someone who has survived the streets of Ohio as well as the walls of death row. Who has the ability to show love and compassion to the daughter he has but, at the same time, grows more and more volatile towards those around him and the system he feels failed him. He talks to me about how kids need a better education in order to get off the streets. He also tells me how he has placed mirrors in his cell so that when he "debates about issues [he] sees on television that makes [him] upset, [he] can look into the mirror as though [he] is debating another person." This bring him peace and is something he has done since he has been locked up. He told me that he does not see this as a mental issue at all but a good way to solve some of his own internal problems. He even goes to such lengths as to make sure that the mirrors he uses in his cell are turned a certain way so that when he sees himself, "They appear distorted enough to make it look like [he] is speaking to another person." He likes to ask me my opinion of things like this due to my educational background in psychology. I will ask him just like I ask all the others when they want to know if the things that they do are normal, "What is normal in your mind?" He has never spoken to anyone about this other than me and thanked me for letting him tell me this.

Cleveland fears being put to death. He never feared going to prison, he never feared taking the lives of others, but he fears being put to death. One of the reasons he reached out to me was because of the past executions I have witnessed and the fact that there are so many things left for them to guess at since it is never really explained to them. They all want to know what to expect. Cleveland, however, wanted to know if he was able to wear something "more comfortable when [he] is executed instead of prison issued clothes." He also wanted to know if the family of the victims are going to be there; and if so, would his daughter be able to hear anything they said about him when he was strapped to the execution bed being put to death. I explained to him that he would indeed have to wear the issued prison uniform they give him; and yes, if the other witnesses say anything, due to the room being so confined, with only a small partition separating the family of the victims and the witnesses he has approved, whatever said will be heard. He decided that he would not invite his daughter then because "I don't want her to hear anything they may or may not say about me." As for the clothes he has to wear when his life ends, he said, "I guess I will have to make do."

As his date grew closer, Cleveland became angrier at the system but also more at peace with himself. He says in one of his letters, "The strange thing is, I'm [be]coming more relaxed about the whole thing day by day, and it's a really calm feeling, and I am able to sleep much better these last few weeks, and I owe you some of that credit because if I didn't have you to talk to with, I'd most likely bottle everything up and shut the world out." You can only imagine how relieved he was when his date was once again pushed back. He is scheduled to die in less than two years and knowing Cleveland Jackson as well as I do, he will once again start to use those mirrors.

Cleveland Jackson and Kimberlin on Ohio's death row.

David Allen has been on death row since 1991 for the robbery and murder of an 84-year-old woman who also ministered to Allen when he was previously incarcerated for sexual battery. He is scheduled to die in April 2023. Although an older man now, Allen still has the ability to put the fear into people. You can see this in his letters, his paintings, and his eyes.

I came to meet Allen in 2006 when he was being housed at the Ohio State Penitentiary death row in Youngstown, Ohio. This was during the time when Ohio had inmates being housed in Youngstown and Mansfield after closing death row in Lucasville. He is currently being housed in Chillicothe, Ohio, where all of the males on death row are being kept until the day before their execution. He is a self-described, self-taught "Bob Ross Painter." He was going on 48 years old when we first spoke and completely grey. He looked to be a lot older at the time, but I guess living on death row does age you quite a bit. He was the type of inmate that one would normally expect to be in the sense that he professed his innocence and was mad as hell at the system for doing him so wrong.

He has since changed his tune. Back then, he told me that he had already lost his mother and his older brother while being locked up and when asked if he was bitter, he stated, "I guess I have to say no; I'm smarter in the area of life and know that being bitter doesn't help a thing." He went on to say that "I don't even want the state compensation should they be honest enough to do the right thing and drop all of the charges against me."

To say that David Allen was arrogant and had this huge sense of entitlement about him would be putting it mildly. He told me that he would really like to talk to me more about his case and to see what I could do for him. He went on to say that since he was one of the best painters and has done ten huge murals for the prison since he got there he would be willing to paint me landscapes in oil because "that's all I do is landscapes in oil." In doing so, he would also answer any of my questions, tell me whatever I wanted to know about death row since he knows everyone on death row personally, and allow me to use any of his information in my book without even asking for a profit share. I could have all of this for two things, "money and packages." I had to explain to Mr. Allen that this is not how I work. I do not assist people on death row to get their convictions overturned and that he needs a lawyer for that. I do not pay guys on death row for their time, letters, or information; and I am not in the business of buying death row art. I would however be willing to buy him art supplies and some food on occasion; but if he was looking for someone to contribute to his lifestyle and legal defense, then he has contacted the wrong person. I respectfully wished him all the best and told him he knew how to contact me if he ever changed his mind on things. I did not hear from him again for a couple of years.

Allen reached out to me one day by sending me some paintings in the mail and asking if I remembered him. He went on to say that he had heard I was still interviewing guys on death row, and I was working on an art book or something and since his appeals were all exhausted, he thought we could start over. I am not exactly sure what caused him to have this change of heart, but I do know that he was no longer professing his innocence, he wasn't asking to be paid for his information; and based on the paintings of skulls, demons, and ghosts, he was also no longer limiting himself to painting landscapes only as he told me before.

Allen is currently 64 years old and a self-described "Sexual Deviant." He has told me that he considers himself a "Tri-Sexual, because I will try anything sexual." Apparently, death row has not diminished his libido either. This is not only evidenced by his written letters but also in his paintings. You see, when people who do not really know what and who they are dealing with when it comes to death row, they can find themselves in very bad situations. I call these people "Hobbyists." They will try to pass themselves off as true crime writers or experts on serial killers or even researchers. They have no formal educational background; they may be "thinking about publishing a book" or any number of things. The fact is, that just because you write an inmate or inmates and you have gotten them to respond or even send you art or they may have watched every murder documentary on television or been to different Crime Cons, it does not make you an expert. Hell, I have a doctorate in psychology, a master's in counseling, and bachelor's degrees in both criminal justice and sociology. I have been doing this for nearly fifteen years and have been called an expert before, yet I still don't claim to be. I say this stuff because David Allen is one of those inmates that loves to suck the "Hobbyists" down his rabbit hole.

At first glance, you see this old man with a shaved head and all white beard. A man who will paint you some of the nicest wildlife and nature scenes you could ever ask for. He will charm you into his world of make believe where he will then entangle you in his web of sorrows and lies. You only realize this after he has taken your money, your time, and your dignity and has moved on to the next person he can so masterfully manipulate. I was lucky enough to stop this from happening to myself, but don't worry, I too have been taken advantage of over the years by other inmates. With David Allen, I was able to prevent this from the very beginning and then allowed him to return to me on my own terms. I accepted his "Bob Ross" style of paintings for a little while and even allowed him to tell me how he was "railroaded" and put on death row for doing nothing wrong. When the letters piled up and the paintings began to take up more space than I felt he was worth, I decided to let him know it was time to stop the masquerade and start talking to me about his true identity. It was going to be this way, or I was done wasting my time with him. He agreed and here we are today.

With a signed document asking me to attend his scheduled execution in hand, we talked about the real David Allen. He is a lonely person who craves attention and sex. While some of his art is amazing to look at, the ones that depict his true self leave little to desire. In fact, many of his paintings would make "most people sick." Not because of what he paints, but what he *uses in his paints*! When he paints me the scenes where he is fantasizing about sexually violating another person or persons, mixed with the white paint on a canvas of black is his own semen. Yes, you read that correctly, he uses his own semen to paint the sex scenes he thinks about. Thinking about sexually violating a woman, a man, a boy, or girl will get him aroused enough for him to be able to masturbate and then paint with his own bodily fluids. (Hopefully, those hobbyists are paying attention as to why death row is no place to go and have fun). Now I have had plenty of death row inmates send me paintings and drawings using human blood before and that is bad enough, but David Allen is the only one (that I am aware of) that has sent me artwork using his own semen. Luckily, he will write me and let me know which paintings he will be doing and when so I can keep an eye out (and gloves on). The only other person I have dealt with over the years who would at least admit to being so sexually deviant while locked away was Samuel Little, but that is another story for later.

Allen would go on to tell me that he was ten years old when he first lost his virginity to a woman. He used to cut grass for people in his neighborhood and one woman who was at least fifty-years-old was unable to pay him when it was time to get paid. I think most would agree that a typical ten-year-old would say that it was all right to pay next time or maybe accept some candy or even tell her not to worry about it. David Allen was not your typical ten-year-old. He did say that she asked him if she could pay him another way, and when she did ask, "My mind went right to her pussy." He remembers it today as "the best fuck I ever had." He would go on to tell me that he told her he wanted to have sex with her and that "she really didn't struggle with it." He says that he knew what he wanted and was not going to let her get out of paying up so he decided this would be her payment. He would continue to cut her grass for sex the rest of the year, and she also introduced him to oral and anal sex as well. He knew then he could control women whenever he wanted. By having sex with her the first time, she would have to continue to have sex with him whenever he wanted; otherwise, he would get her into trouble. He was also savvy enough to not go around telling others about it because he knew they would say something to others, and it would end. This would lead him into a life of sexual encounters that to this day he loves to talk about. Man or woman, it did not matter to David. He would tell me how he would have sex with women for money where he would pay them, and there were plenty of times where he would have sex with men where they would pay him. "Oral, anal, threesomes, or more-somes, I enjoyed them all." It did not matter if he needed the money or not, he was willing to do anything and everything sexually.

Lucky for me my wife (Wendy) has thick skin and has been with me throughout this adventure since day one because David Allen, like so many others on death row—Scott Peterson, Charles Ng, Brandy Jennings, Cherrie Rhoads, just to name a few—will always ask about her. Allen, on the other hand, goes above and beyond just asking about her. He will fantasize about her sexually and send his "special paintings" with a full description of what he was thinking about when he painted them. Again, one more reason why people out there just thinking about writing about a killer need to stop and think what is at stake. They will know about you and your entire family one way or another, and they will let you know. When someone out there decides to contact a serial killer or mass murderer thinking it would be cool to talk to them or get them to write, think again. You are being selfish by putting others at risk. We all have internet access, and so do they. That means my wife has to put up with not just the letters that arrive in the mail; but the artwork laying around, the e-mails, and the phone calls. This does not include the emotional toll it may take on the spouse or loved ones of having death row inmates across the country knowing where they live, work, and what they like to do for entertainment. You may just want to re-think that next post before you put it on Facebook or Instagram because they see that too when they want. They know where you go and whom you are with each time you post it. She accepted this many years ago knowing this was not something that I was doing for fun but for a real purpose. I still see the look in her eyes from time to time when her name comes out of the mouth of a serial killer, and I can't help but to feel awful for her. She has accepted this life, but she never asked for it.

Letter from David Allen inviting me to his execution in Ohio along with a painting on canvas.

*David Allen's painting on canvas using
his own semen to paint with.*

David Allen was able to survive different execution
dates, different death rows throughout Ohio, and was even
on his death bed this past year when he was transported
to The Ohio State University Hospital after contracting
COVID-19. I had other inmates write to me to tell me that
Allen was taken off death row to the hospital and that he
would not be coming back. In true David Allen form, he not

only made a full recovery, but he was back to his old self of painting and talking about his sexual excursions that he so dearly misses. He does not say much about his victim these days. I suspect he is hoping for that last minute stay from the clemency board as his time nears once again; but rest assured, he is not remorseful in any way.

Usually writers of non-fiction/true crime have their "inside sources" who provide them with the information that they want or need. Most times they are in the form of police officers, retired detectives, or even prison guards. I guess I am no different other than the fact that my inside source also happens to be sitting on death row. His name is Charles (Chuck) Lorraine, and he was sentenced to die in Ohio's electric chair in 1986 for the brutal murders of an elderly couple that he was supposed to was hired to help out. Mr. Montgomery was seventy-seven years old and was stabbed five times while his wife, age eighty, was stabbed nine times. Mrs. Montgomery was bedridden and unable to walk as Lorraine repeatedly stabbed them with their own kitchen knife and robbed them (Nexstar Media Inc. 2021). He is patiently awaiting his date with death, which is scheduled for March 15, 2023.

I came to know Chuck though another inmate, Fred Treesh, whose execution I had witnessed several years ago. Fred had asked me to look after him when he was gone and said that he could be a good person to talk to about others. Lorraine reached out to me after Fred's death, and we have talked ever since. When you think of a person who may have no conscience, no ability to show remorse, and no respect for human life you need not think any further than Charles Lorraine. Not only did he slaughter this lovely couple in their golden years, but he also robbed them, went to the local bar to drink and brag about killing an old couple, and then, to add insult to it all, went back to the home to show a friend and to steal more of their possessions (Jennifer Rodrigues, Oct. 15. 2019, WKBN). Lorraine was a hired handyman for the elderly couple, who trusted him with everything they owned. In his own words, "They were two of the nicest people you would ever want to meet" (Jennifer Rodrigues, Oct. 15. 2019, WKBN). When I think of Chuck, I think of the character "Red" played by Morgan Freeman in *The Shawshank Redemption.*

Chuck likes to be known as the person who can get you what you want on death row. At least for me anyways. He prides himself on being able to supply me with information about other guys on death row, and he will send a "kite" to certain inmates that he thinks should have my name and address to contact me to talk to. That is how I came to know David Allen. Chuck had sent a kite to Allen to contact me and send me some art. (A kite, by the way, is a note that is passed from one inmate to the next, to the next, in the form of a little folded piece of paper containing a written note). Lorraine also tried to act as a mediator for myself and Anthony Sowell when we stopped speaking. It amazes me how some of these guys will go to great lengths to try to get everyone to get along, yet they have no regard for the human lives they took.

Not known for his artistic ability, Lorraine seems to find the ones on death row who are either good at painting or good at talking. When he finds someone, who passes his test of being a "stand-up guy," he will then provide them with my name and address and have them write me and send me stuff. Often, if I decide I want to interview them, I will respond in letter form, and then they end up sending me a visitation form to complete where they have already approved me to see them in person. Prior to me ever receiving anything from those he sends my way, Chuck will e-mail me and tell me who and what to expect, the complete history of the guy, and if I should be able to trust him or not. On more than a few occasions, Chuck has written me to let me know that he has given my information to a guy and that I should "watch out for him" because he is not sure if he really trusts him or not. I find it humorous that a death row inmate has to almost "vet" my guys before they have permission to talk to me. The sad part about it is that he is usually correct in his assessments of them. Other inmates will also let me know when another person wants to have me interview them, but they will usually ask me if it is all right to pass my name on to them, and that is about all. Chuck has always gone that extra mile in order to keep me around, I guess. When a guy decides to try and play me for a food box or for art supplies in his first letter before I even talk to them and I let Chuck know, he seems to almost beat himself up over sending me a bad apple. Again, from the psychological aspect of it all, it is astonishing that a death row inmate is more concerned about not upsetting me than he was about killing an innocent, elderly couple. I always joke with my friends and family that at least I have people on death row who have my back.

Dear Bill,   6-6-2021

How are you my friend? I pray that you are doing well.
As for myself i am doing good. I'd be a lot better if i didn't
have this execution date over my head, which is what i want
to talk to you about.
I would like to ask you if you would be one of the three
witnesses to my execution? It's still some time aways but
i would like to make sure the paper work here is done
and that everything is in place when that time comes.
My execution date is set for March of 2023.
We have been friends now for some years and i know you have
been to witness other executions of inmates on Ohio's death
row. Many of us know you have tried to help us and be there
for us and it would mean a lot if you would be there on that
day. Back in 2012 in January when i almost got executed you
were on my witness list to that execution but i was given a
stay of execution, but it meant a lot that you were there when
i needed you. Thanks buddy.
Well feel free to write anytime and thank you for being such a
great friend.   Chuck

Charles L. Lorraine
#A-194-013

Letter from Charles Lorraine inviting me to his execution in Ohio. (see full resolution letters and forms at **wbp.bz/wmdgallery***)*

What Has Death Row Done to Me?

I have been asked so many questions over the years about everything you can imagine about death row since I began this journey a lifetime ago. Are you ever afraid of them? Are you worried they will find you and your family one day? What is an execution like? And of course, can I go with you to the next one? (That question always gets me). It is not like it is a sporting event that you need to score tickets to go see. It certainly is not for the faint of heart; and while almost everyone says that they would love to see one, I find it hard to imagine that they would ever really be able to sit through one and not suffer long-term emotional effects from it afterwards. It is after all, a state sanctioned murder! Yes, they are evil; yes, they are there for a reason; but in the end, they are a human being who has done nothing wrong to me or my loved ones. They have taught me so much over the years. How to get inside of their minds, what each day is like living on death row, what makes them want to kill, and they have certainly taught me more about myself.

I never in a million years thought that I would find myself sitting face to face with a serial killer (let alone many serial killers), listening to them while taking notes about how long it would take them to squeeze the life out of another human, or what it is like to watch their victim's life slowly disappear as they twist a knife inside of their body. Never did I think that I would be asking another person what it is like to hear the sounds of bones breaking, or what it felt like to be having intercourse with the corpse of the person they just killed. Men, women, children. Family members, friends, strangers. No human was off limits to so many of these killers it seemed. It has desensitized me.

I will sometimes watch these crime shows on television with my wife, and she will even laugh when a person is talking, and they seem to always say, "This is the most evil person I have ever come across in my entire legal or law enforcement career." That killer they are speaking about may have killed a couple of people or was involved in multiple rapes and killed a person. My wife even knows it has changed me because when she laughs, she is looking directly at me waiting to see what my response will be. It's changed her as well. She has known me our entire life. She has been on this bizarre journey just as long as I have. In fact, she has dropped me off more times than I can count to death rows all over the country and has picked me up after I was done with each one. She knows it has changed us without even saying it. In the beginning, just writing to a couple of death row inmates or receiving a painting in the mail would get me excited to where I had to sit down and write that person back right then. Today, I can look in my office (our daughter's old bedroom) and see 30-40 letters never even opened yet. Gone are the days where our son and daughter would want to see the different styles of artwork sent to me from guys who killed people and them being fascinated by their work. Instead, on the dining room table, along with an office downtown and our daughter and son's bedrooms, sits over 1,200 pieces of death row art from all over the country just laying around. My wife can now almost instantly look at a piece of art and, before she sets her purse and keys on top of it, know exactly which killer painted it, drew it, or folded it into whatever shape or size it is. It would be an understatement to say that no piece of death row mail even solicits an excited response these days from her or the kids.

Now when I receive an e-mail or phone call from a death row inmate who requests me to interview them, the first thing I usually do is see how many people they have killed; and, if it is just one or two, I find it difficult to even respond. What does that say about me? Have I become so "jaded" that a murder of another human being doesn't even cause me to raise an eyebrow? It's sad enough that our very own society has witnessed so many mass shootings over the years that many just turn the channel to put it out of their minds; now I see myself looking the other way whenever I hear about a murder. Not just hearing about a murder but discarding a letter written by the very hands that took another person's life. I do not see myself as being insensitive towards others when I do look the other way or ignore some who reach out to me from death row, but I do think that I have become sort of "numb" to the fact that society seems to glamorize serial killers or mass murderers who reside on death row. The way the media sensationalizes them on every documentary produced does not help the cause either; however by me writing about them, telling their stories, and displaying their art, one could argue that I am a no better. We all have choices in this world. The choices made by those I have spoken to over the years have landed them where they are right now, waiting for their final walk to the death chamber. I could choose to walk away and never return to Ohio's death row, to witness anymore executions, or to interview anymore condemned killers; or I could choose to continue to do what I have become so skilled at doing over the years. Maybe even branch out some and learn from others on death rows across the country and see where that takes me next.

Where Do I Go from Here?

The last couple of years have been challenging for all of us. We have all bear witness to the devastation that the onset of the worldwide pandemic of COVID-19 has brought upon us. Not only in the number of deaths but also the crippling standstill of the nation's entertainment, transportation, educational system, health care system, and even being able to be close to our loved ones. This also brought on the complete shutdown of visitations within the prison system across the country as well. In fact, at the time of this writing, the only death row that has opened back up for me to continue my interviews has been Florida's. This has allowed many death row inmates to use other means of communications such as Zoom, writing, e-mails, phone calls, and in art form. What it does not allow is for me to be able to see their actions as they tell me how they committed their murders or look into their eyes to see if I can tell how they are really feeling as they speak. It does not allow me to gauge their emotional reaction when they talk about their family or friends (if they have any) or hear what they really have to say but are too afraid to put it in writing.

What I do know is that those states that still currently have the death penalty seem to be keeping it in their grasps. States like South Carolina who just passed legislation to adopt the electric chair as well as the firing squad as the method of choice given to the condemned inmate when lethal drugs are unavailable goes to show that some states refuse to let go of this concept of punishment. Idaho, Texas, Florida, and Tennessee are among other states who at the time of this writing are also scheduling inmates to die. While it may be true that during the year of the pandemic we saw a huge decline in the use of the death penalty, (with the exception of the Federal Government), now that the mandates on this virus are lessening, the scheduling of executions are resuming. I believe that starting at the end of 2021 and into 2022, we as a country will see the use of capital punishment beginning to surge.

What remains to be seen is how these executions will be carried out. New methods, new protocols, perhaps less transparency? This was the case when Texas resumed their executions in May 2021. On May 19, 2021, Texas executed their first inmate in nearly a year, but something very strange took place. According to Juan A. Lozano and Michael Graczyk of the Associated Press, Quintin Jones was put to death by a lethal dose of pentobarbital in Huntsville, Texas. The execution took only twelve minutes according to prison officials and was carried out without any glitches. Jones also made a brief last statement saying, "I was so glad to leave this world a better, more positive place," and also according to prison officials, he stated, "I hope I left everyone a plate of food full of happy memories, happiness, and no sadness." It was not strange that Texas executated another inmate on death row: they are known for that. It was not strange that Texas Governor Gregg Abbott declined to stay the execution: he had only done so one time since being elected in 2015. What made this execution so different was the fact that Texas had executed 570 inmates prior to Quintin Jones since it resumed executions in 1982, and all 570 executions were carried out with media witnesses present. Oddly, there were no media present for this one. According to officials, this execution included a number of new personnel who had never participated in the process before. They then apologized and said that it would be investigated and not happen again (Lozano and Graczyk, AP-Texas, May 20, 2021). Still, this has to make people question what the future of capital punishment will look like in the coming years.

Brandy Jennings and Kimberlin on Florida's death row.

HEY DOC BILL,   9/8/21

SO, WHAT WOULD YOU THINK ABOUT BEING A WITNESS AT
MY STATE SPONSORED MURDER (EXECUTION), IF THEY EVER
SCHEDULE ME?

I WAS THINKING IT MIGHT BE A LITTLE COMFORTING
KNOWING AT LEAST ONE SET OF EYES IN THE AUDIENCE
DON'T HATE ME FOR WHAT I DID NOT DO. YOU SHOULD ALSO
KNOW THAT IF IT EVER COMES TO BE AND I HAVE ANY
SAY SO IT WILL BE CARRIED OUT BY ELECTRICUTION AND
NOT LEATHAL INJECTION. TO DIE OR BE MURDERED LIKE A
JUNKY ON HIS BACK AND A NEEDLE IN HIS ARM IS NOT
FOR ME. I'VE NEVER BEEN A JUNKEE AND SUCH A DISRESPECT
JUST RUBS ME WRONG. I THOUGHT YOU SHOULD KNOW THAT
YOU ALSO MIGHT LIKE TO KNOW THAT IF I HAVE TO GO
BY WAY OF INJELTION YOU MIGHT NOT WANT TO BE THERE AS
I AM GOING TO CURSE EVERY SOUL PRESENT WITH MY DIEING
BREATH. NO GUARANTEE I'LL BE IN THE WRITE MIND TO
EXCLUDE YOU.

WELL THAT ABOUT COVERS IT MY FRIEND AND LET ME
KNOW YOUR ANSWER AFTER YOU'VE THOUGHT ABOUT IT. ALSO
ANOTHER QUESTION.

IF PUSH COMES TO SHOVE, WOULD YOU BE INTERESTED IN
DISPOSING OF MY REMAINS? SOMETHING TO THINK ABOUT
AND THERE IS NO RUSH.

ALOT TO THINK ABOUT SO I WILL LEAVE YOU FOR NOW
WITH BEST WISHES TO YOU AND ALL YOUR LOVED ONES.

                              WELL IF YOU FED
                              ME BETTER IT WOULD
                              NOT SMELL OR LOOK
                              LIKE THAT
                              Crazy Bill Dan

*Letter from Brandy Jennings inviting me to his
execution by electrocution in Florida.*

ABOUT THE AUTHOR

Author Bill Kimberlin, Psy.D. has been researching and writing about death row and the execution process for well over a decade. He earned a Bachelor of Science degree in Criminal Justice, a Master of Arts degree in Counseling, and a Doctorate in Psychology. He began his Postdoctoral Residency in Psychology but decided to focus more on the criminal minds of those who have decided to devote their lives to the killings of innocent human beings which led them to death row. Kimberlin is married to his wife (Wendy) of 30 years and has two amazing children, Bailey and Mackenzie. His family has been the backbone to his never-ending research, and they have been there for him throughout his journey. Kimberlin grew up in Ohio where his father, (Jay) still resides. His Mother, (Etta), to whom this book is dedicated to, passed away in December of 2020. He has one older brother, (Jay jr.) who also resides in Ohio. Bill and Wendy currently reside in Florida where they enjoy the sun while continuing to work in their fields of study. He continues to travel to different death rows across the country interviewing both male and female death row inmates and has been asked to witness several more executions in various states in the near future.

Dedicated to my mother, Etta S. Kimberlin.
09/1940-12/2020

Works Cited

"Article 3: Freedom from Torture and Inhuman or Degrading Treatment." Article 3: Freedom from Torture and Inhuman or Degrading Treatment | Equality and Human Rights Commission, 3 June 2021, www.equality-humanrights.com/en/human-rights-act/article-3-freedom-torture-and-inhuman-or-degrading-treatment.

"Death Penalty Fast Facts." CNN, Cable News Network, July 9 2021, www.cnn.com/2013/07/19/us/death-penalty-fast-facts/index.html.

"Death Penalty Information Center." Idealist, www.idealist.org/en/nonprofit-job/6eff3763960a4236b38cb146f40840de-data-fellow-death-penalty-information-center-washington.

"Description of Each Execution Method." Death Penalty Information Center, Aug. 1, 2021, deathpenaltyinfo.org/executions/methods-of-execution/description-of-each-method.

"Facts." Death Penalty Focus, Dec. 18, 2020, deathpenalty.org/facts/.

"Lockup: Raw : Msnbcw : October 4, 2014 2:00AM-2:31AM Pdt : Free Borrow & Streaming." Internet Archive, Aug. 1, 2021, archive.org/details/MSNBCW_20141004_090000_Lockup_Raw.

Memmott, Mark. "No More Special Last Meals for Death Row Inmates in Texas." NPR, Sept. 23, 2011, www.npr.org/sections/thetwo-way/2011/09/23/140735845/no-more-special-last-meals-for-death-row-inmates-in-texas.

Mueller, Benjamin. "Death of Obese Ohio Inmate ESCALATES Death Penalty Debate." Los

Angeles Times, Los Angeles Times,Aug. 7, 2013, www.latimes.com/nation/la-xpm-2013-aug-07-la-na-nn-ronald-post-ohio-20130806-story.html.

"ODRC > HOME." ODRC, 2012, www.drc.ohio.gov/.

"Ohio Revised Code." Ohio Revised Code | Ohio Laws, Anderson, 2019, codes.ohio.gov/orc/.

The Ohio State Reformatory Preservation Society. "The Ohio State Reformatory Experience." The Ohio State Reformatory, 2018, www. mrps.org/.

"Ohio." Death Penalty Information Center, July 19, 2021, deathpenalty-info.org/state-and-federal-info/state-by-state/ohio.

"Send Packages to Inmates Incarcerated in Correctional Facilities." Walkenhorst's, 2020, walkenhorsts.com/.

"States with the Death Penalty, Death Penalty Bans, and Death Penalty Moratoriums - Death Penalty - Procon.org." Death Penalty, 25 Mar. 2021, deathpenalty.procon.org/states-   with-the-death-penalty-and-states-with-death-penalty-bans/.

Welsh-Higgins, Andrew. "Sitting on Death Row, Inmates Complain about Birds." The Advocate, AP, May 19, 2014, www. www.newarkad-vocate.com/story/news/2014/05/19/report-birds-an-issue-in-ohio-death-row-cells/9289341/.

Made in United States
Orlando, FL
13 February 2022

14771571R00074